How To Sell Your Inventions For Cash

Second Edition
Revised

Mike Rounds

CPM Systems ❧ Rancho Palos Verdes, California, U.S.A.

How To Sell Your Inventions For Cash
Mike Rounds

Published by:

SYSTEMS
PUBLISHING COMPANY
6318 Ridgepath Court
Rancho Palos Verdes, CA 90275-3248
mailto:CPMPub@aol.com

This edition is an expansion and revision of a work previously published as *Inventing For Money*, copyright © 1997 by Nancy Miller and Michael F. Rounds and *How to Sell Your Ideas and Inventions . . . for cash*, copyright © 1991, 1992, 1994, and 1996 both by published by CPM Systems

Printed in the United States of America
Revised 2004 Reprinted 2007

ISBN 1-891440-27-6

            Library of Congress Cataloging-in-Publication Data

Rounds, Mike.
   How to sell your inventions for cash / Mike Rounds.-- 2nd ed., rev.
        p. cm.
   Includes bibliographical references (p.   ) and index.
   Rev. ed. of: Inventing for money.
   ISBN 1-891440-27-6 (pbk.)
 1. New products. 2. Inventions. 3. Patents. 4. Copyright--
Royalties. I. Rounds, Mike. Inventing for money. II. Title.

   HF5415.153.R69 2004
   658.5'75--dc22

2004011146

Table of Contents

Warning—Disclaimer

How to Sell Your Inventions for Cash is designed to provide information on the invention licensing process and the topics related to it. It is sold with the understanding that the publisher and author are not engaged in rendering legal, accounting or other professional services. If expert assistance is required, the services of a competent professional should be sought.

It is not the purpose of *How to Sell Your Inventions for Cash* to reprint all the information that is otherwise available to inventors, but instead to complement, amplify, and supplement other texts. You are urged to read all the available material, learn as much as possible about both the inventing and marketing of new inventions, and tailor the information to your individual needs. For more information, see the many resources in Appendix on page 135.

Inventing is not a get-rich-quick scheme. Anyone who decides to invent and license their inventions must expect to invest time and effort into it. For many people, inventing is more lucrative than becoming a manufacturer.

Every effort has been made to be as complete and as accurate as possible. However, there *may be mistakes*, both typographical and in content. Therefore, this text should be used only as a general guide and not as the ultimate source of current inventions and marketing information. Furthermore, this book contains information on intellectual property law and Internet resources that are current only up to the published date.

The purpose of this book is to educate and entertain. The author and CPM Systems shall have neither liability nor responsibility to any person or entity with respect to any loss or damage caused, or alleged to have been caused, directly or indirectly, by the information contained in *How to Sell Your Inventions for Cash*.

If you do not wish to be bound by the above, you may return this book to the publisher for a full refund, except when required as part of a course's material fee.

Chapter 1
The Creative Process

Since the first cave dweller attached a rock to a stick to form a crude hammer, humans have been coming up with new ideas and inventions to make their lives easier and more productive.

The reality of creativity is that it's something that occurs because human beings get bored, tired, hungry, or frustrated and decide that there should be a different way of accomplishing something. This different way is called creativity or inventiveness.

In today's rapidly changing world, creativity and inventiveness are not an option or a luxury—they're a way of life. Current statistics coupled with our own experiences, tell us that products, services, and occupations are changing and evolving at an ever-increasing rate.

The good news is that the rapidity of change creates tremendous opportunities for creative people to develop new solutions. The bad news is that the old adage, *he who hesitates is lost*, has never been truer. If you question this, think about the ideas and inventions that you've had and then seen in stores or catalogs. Frustrating, isn't it?

We live in a world where creativity is not only recognized, but also prized and rewarded. The key is to determine the best way for you, as a creative individual, to exploit your creativity and obtain the greatest reward possible.

How to Sell Your Inventions for Cash is about understanding the creative process and what you can do to get others to reward you for that creativity.

Before you can understand and exploit the process of marketing your creativity for a profit, you should understand the different terms used in exploiting the creative process.

Since our language is dynamic, rather than static, constant usage of terms cause their meanings to become distorted or misunderstood. So that we are on the same page, here is how we have defined these words. There is a dichotomy in the creative process. It is more of an *either/or* tradeoff than a black and white process. If you're going to get involved with inventing for money it's probably a good idea to know what your odds of success are and where you think you want to fit into the process.

Creativity

Merriam-Webster defines creativity as the quality of being creative or the ability to create. For example, if you have a new idea for a vehicle tire and develop the idea into a working product, you have engaged in the creative process.

Further, Merriam-Webster defines productivity as the quality or state of being productive. If you work on a tire assembly line, you produce lots and lots of tires for vehicles. Your work output is both valuable and highly productive. However, it is NOT considered creative because you utilize the ideas and original thoughts of others.

The value of an original idea is not always represented by the amount of money involved or the profits derived because of its success.

First, there are three reasons to be creative:

1. To fill an immediate need. For example, if you are manufacturing a steel table and discover that you need something to hold the parts in place while they are being welded and you don't have the holding fixture, you might decide to build something that is easy to set up, use, and can be adapted to lots of other projects as well.

2. For fun. Many people build things, paint, and modify exiting products to make them more suitable for their needs because it's enjoyable and they get the benefits from the improvements immediately following the work.

3. For profit. This is where you are compensated in some form of payment other than personal satisfaction. It may seem overly simplistic but if you're not being compensated for your creativity, you're inventing for one of the first two reasons. You can justify it any way you want, but the results will point out that you're not doing it for money.

   Bear in mind that there's nothing wrong with NOT being paid for your creativity—it's simply not lucrative.

Some of the cleverest and most useful things in the world have been created because somebody was having fun or because they needed a better, faster, or different way to do something. The fact that the inventor didn't receive any money for them did not reduce their value as useful ideas.

Ideas

Turning to Merriam-Webster again, we find that an idea is a formulated thought or opinion. An invention is a product of the imagination, a device, contrivance, or process originated after study and experiment.

Ideas are highly marketable in the form of consulting services or as an employee who gets paid to think up new methods, processes, and programs to be implemented by others. These individuals are usually not involved with the actual physical implementation of the ideas but may ultimately be responsible for their success through the management and financial processes of business.

How to Sell Your Inventions for Cash is about the concept of inventions and the process of inventing. Ideas that have not been embodied or consulting services are not considered here. If you consider yourself a consultant and want to sell your expertise without embodying it in the form of a physical product, the book *Marketing the One Person Business* covers those topics.

Inventions

Everything starts with an idea and inventions become the physical embodiment of an idea.

Inventions are usually only saleable after the idea has been embodied in physical or usable form. This means that if you are going to be a successful inventor you not only have to think of a new idea but you also have to produce a prototype to prove that the idea works. This is called a *proof of concept* model and is where you go to your workshop and build your idea into something that does what you say it will do or hire someone to build it for you.

Employee

An employee is defined as "one employed by another usually for wages or salary and in a position below the executive level."

In today's competitive world, the chances of you getting a job doing creative work that you excel at are about one in five or 20 percent. This means that for purely economic reasons (you take the job because you gotta eat) that the odds are 5:1 that you'll end up working on projects that have little or nothing to do with your strongest skills or interests.

Once you get a job doing creative work, the chances of your ideas being utilized by the firm are about one in five or 20 percent. This is due to organizational policies that require the review of a variety of choices or approaches and statistically yours are not going to be accepted more than one time out of five times. As an employee your ideas have a four percent chance of getting from your drawing board to the marketplace (1/5 of 20 percent).

This is consistent with the standard statement made by companies when they are asked their success rate. The standard answer is generally, "1 in 20 make it to market."

> "Less than five percent of all new ideas ever result in a new product or service, and less than ten percent of those that do are successful."
>
> Michael LeBoeuf, author of Fast Forward

Incidentally, of the products that make it to market, only 20 percent of them are financially successful, making the final success percentage for a new idea a little less than one percent.

This is a solid argument for being an employee and leaving the risks of success to the organization because as an employee, you'll be paid even when the odds of success are low.

Of course, there's always that time when something that you've developed for someone else takes off and makes them a bazillion dollars. Your reward is usually limited to the salary (and maybe a bonus) you were paid because the higher the risk, the higher the reward, and the risk was theirs, not yours.

Manufacturers

Manufacturing is to make a product suitable for use, to make from raw materials by hand or by machinery, or to produce according to an organized plan and with division of labor.

For example, if you own a machine shop, you may be called upon to build a metal table from steel. The idea has already been proven and you will be creating clones or copies of a proven design for sale.

In return for your efforts, when the product is completed and approved by the client, you send the client an invoice for the goods and services and then you receive payment.

Research and Development Groups

Prior to the industrial revolution in the late 1800's, independent individuals conducted most of the creative work in the world. They would work privately, secretly, and diligently to produce new products and processes that would make their world a better and more productive place.

To be successful, these creative individuals would, out of necessity, need to be competent businesspersons in addition to creative individuals to commercialize their ideas and get their ideas into use. Rarely did these individuals ever work in teams during the initial development and business start-up stage.

One of Thomas Edison's greatest inventions was the research team. He is credited with being the first person in history to formally organize a group of individuals into a research and development group.

Following Edison's establishment of the research team, many organizations established internal development teams to develop new ideas and innovations into commercially viable products and services.

This new concept did not eliminate the need for independent inventors but it did add a new dimension to the craft—creativity by contract. Since Edison's time, we have established a world that grows and changes in an almost incomprehensible time frame because organizations and their research teams as well as independently creative individuals are developing new ideas at an exponential rate.

The industrial revolution offered people a choice to remain independent and entrepreneurial or become employed by an organization in return for wages and benefits. The effect of industrialization is that the bulk of the world's inventiveness is captive to an existing organization that has the resources to pay for both the development and the exploitation of new ideas for profit.

Individuals who engage in this form of creativity are designers, engineers, architects or scientists. Technically, these individuals are all inventors and their work is termed work-for-hire and belongs to the organization that pays for the work.

The law says that the work created by the individual for the organization belongs to the organization, not the individual, because the organization bought and paid for it just as though they had purchased a physical object. Most creative people prefer employment because it allows them the latitude of being compensated to maintain a decent lifestyle even when their ideas are unsuccessful, a part of the invention process which is unavoidable.

The alternative to being an employee is to operate as an independent inventor, solve an existing problem or fill an obvious need, and then exploit the solution for profit.

Manufacturers get their ideas from two places—in-house developers and designers and independent designers and inventors.

The thing about being an outsider is that you're an outsider, and that puts you in a different position than an in-house designer who can usually get his or her idea reviewed by someone with the authority to proceed with the development and marketing processes.

Invention marketing companies will allude to having inside connections no matter what industry you're specializing in. Based on virtually zero results from these organizations, it appears that it isn't even close to being true—it's an outright lie. We'll touch more on the invention marketing scams in Chapter 10.

No matter what anyone tells you, consider that there are two, and only two ways, which you as an outsider can use to get your idea reviewed by a firm who has the potential of exploiting the idea for you:

1. Know someone inside the firm who can, and will, champion your idea from inside the firm for you.

2. Seek out every firm you can find who deals in the kind of innovations you've created, and see if they're interested in your idea. This is known as cold calling in some industries, but is generically called solicitation and market research.

Entrepreneur

An entrepreneur is defined as "one who organizes, manages, and assumes the risks of a business or enterprise." Entrepreneurs are inventors of businesses who own and operate them for some period following their creation.

The statistics on becoming an entrepreneur and exploiting your own inventions for profit are not very encouraging.

This assumes that you've been able to locate financing for your enterprise and the current funding statistics show that only about one percent of all business plans gets properly funded.

After you achieve funding status, regardless of whether you get it from an outside source or dip into your life savings, reality says if you start a small business, you will probably lose your shirt. One out of three business start-ups fail within six months.

The chances of your product being successful is still one in five and if you make it through the critical first six months, you will have a 25 percent chance of lasting five years.

During the critical start-up and gestation periods, you'll probably end up working 16 hours a day and the cash flow and logistics problems will fall on your shoulders.

There are inventors turned entrepreneurs who have figured out the number of hours spent, the money they received, the grief and anxiety that they've endured they'd have made more money with fewer headaches flippin' burgers.

Becoming a small business and selling what you invented however may lead us to believe the dream is really a nightmare in disguise. Although you can succeed, here are the major reasons why many of the start-up companies based on inventor's new ideas actually fail:

1. Even though you may be highly knowledgeable about engineering and manufacturing, in addition to creating innovative items, building production quantities of products in a start-up factory can be financially draining. If you already had access to these facilities, it would probably be a viable option. Otherwise, you almost have to solicit and obtain subcontract manufacturing, potentially in a third world country where the costs are much lower than in the United States (US).

2. Subcontract manufacturing in third world countries, although significantly lower in cost, is not without its pitfalls and expenses. A solid working knowledge of how business is conducted in the selected country is an integral part of the process and having a reliable and trusted associate who speaks the language and lives in the selected country is a mandate. People with an extensive background in this area can *set 'em up* but the costs are high and the time investment is even higher.

3. Subcontracting still carries with it the cost of production design, production tooling, and a large investment in inventory in order to keep the unit pricing low. Once the manufacturing is complete, there is international shipping, customs and duties, freight forwarding, domestic shipping, warehousing, storage, and inventory control before the business of marketing and promotion even begin.

4. There is a large investment of time as well as money involved in starting and running this kind of business, and the return on your investment of time may or may not happen rapidly enough to make it worth your while to take time from other activities that are more productive. You can always hire people to perform the work but once again, you are looking at more front-end capital and the lengthy return on investment involved.

5. The critical factor in a start-up business is the overhead and operating costs as they pertain to overall profits. Small firms with low-cost products have a difficult time surviving because of the cost to do business. It takes a considerable amount of investment to sell a $5 item that nets a 25-cent profit. If you have hundreds or thousands of items that have this characteristic, you can amortize the daily operating costs throughout the product lines. When overhead has to be carried by one small item, the cost of sales and the overhead costs far outweigh the actual cost of the product and seldom will the consumer pay a price that's high enough to cover your total requirements and still allow you to make a profit.

6. The last, and definitely the most significant factor, is the marketing of the product. Every successful industry has its channel power chain where the marketing and distribution have already been established and operate effectively and efficiently. The time and money involved in either creating a new chain or breaking into an existing chain are significant and requires a working knowledge of that industry's marketing, sales, and distribution network. Knowledgeable and experienced personnel can be hired, but the costs may be far too high to consider. The time to

establish these relationships might be so extensive that your product might not enter the market in a timely manner.

Independent Inventor

An inventor is defined as "one who devises by thinking or produces for the first time through the use of the imagination or of ingenious thinking and experiment." Inventors and other creative people engage in the dual processes of creativity and productivity whereas employees engage solely in productivity.

Becoming an independent inventor, by our own definition, is the *great American dream* and still comes true. It is, however, not the most expeditious route for all creative people to take because inventors are more interested in the creative process than in running a successful business.

Licensing

A licensing agreement is a partnership between an intellectual property rights owner (licensor) and another who is authorized to use such rights (licensee) in exchange for an agreed payment (fee or royalty). A variety of such licensing agreements are available, which may be broadly categorized as follows:

1. Technology License Agreement

2. Trademark Licensing and Franchising Agreement

3. Copyright License Agreement

For example, most authors are good at writing and are not interested in the business side. To be successful, authors license their writings to publishers. The publisher does the printing, marketing, and distribution of the book.

Licensors (the author) enter into a contractual arrangement with the licensee (the publisher) and agree to be compensated in the form of a percentage of the sale. This is known as a royalty and is received after the licensee has sold the items.

Licensing embodies the best of all worlds—remaining an independent inventor and capitalizing on the existing world of manufacturing and distribution.

As mentioned previously, this is what authors have done to see that their written works are given the circulation necessary to make them rich, famous, and allow them to continue doing what they're good at doing—writing—NOT running a business.

Just like authors that have to collect rejection slips before they find a publisher to publish and distribute their work, inventors must follow an almost parallel path to be successful.

To be successful at getting your innovations to the public, you're dealing with warm blooded, mouth breathing, calorie-ingesting entities, called human beings.

When looking at the possibilities for success in involving others in the innovations you've created, the two most important human character traits to be acknowledged and understood are:

1. Human beings resist change. We invest our time and efforts to become familiar with a product or a way of doing things and it's an encroachment on our lives to have to relearn something or to make a change. The result is that we inherently justify that it's much easier to leave things the way they are.

    If you're saying to yourself "logically, that doesn't make sense," you're not alone and logic doesn't necessarily come into play. History shows us that some of the greatest innovations were suppressed because people didn't want to acknowledge that the newer precepts were more accurate or useful because they would have to change.

    Look at the concept of the "flat earth." Christopher Columbus wasn't the first person to believe the world was round. Astronomers and other scientists who predated him had known the realities for centuries. For the kings and rulers, it was much simpler to believe that the world they controlled, or hoped to control, could be represented on a flat table with heavy lines surrounding their piece of that world. To acknowledge that the world was round would have meant that they were not in as much control as they would like to have believed they were.

2. NIH or *not invented here*, an inherent quality of the human psyche is constantly with us. Consider that human beings are the highest form of animal life on planet Earth and all animals are inherently territorial. Whenever something new is presented to us that was not originated by us, either directly or by people under our direct supervision, we revert to a territorial position and begin to defend what we believe is our proprietary territory.

    Even though the new idea might be highly beneficial, the natural process of human nature initially takes over and causes reaction instead of an educated response. Primitive individuals never get over the basic animal response and resist change with as much power as they can.

    Enlightened persons experience the initial tendency to reject the newness of ideas but education, training, and experience allows them the latitude of getting past the basic instincts and intelligently evaluating the merits of alternative thinking.

    What this means to you, as a creative individual, is that no matter what you develop or how valuable it may be, there are going to be individuals who, because of their very nature, will not accept your ideas because it violates their *territorial mindset*.

Your only choice is to move on to another organization that has a more open, enlightened approach to reviewing and accepting change. Then, and only then will you be in a position to mutually exploit your innovations for profit.

This is probably the best of all worlds because it allows you the latitude of working on your own projects, taking minimal risks, and being an integral part of the rewards process if the product becomes wildly successful.

The licensing process for inventors is just as flexible as it is for authors because you can be a part-time or full-time inventor. In other words, you don't have to relinquish the security of your day job to pursue success in another area of interest or expertise.

The only thing you have to watch out for is *conflict of interest*. This means that your independent inventing efforts cannot be related to what your employer is paying you to do.

Current laws stipulate that if you are being paid to do creative work of a specifically defined nature, like original designs, the employer has the rights to the creative process connected with the specific efforts regardless of whether you are on the employer's premises or at home in your hot tub.

The law also states that if you create something and your employer rejects it, you do NOT have the rights to exploit it on your own or sell it someone else. They paid for it and they have the right to do with it as they see fit.

In addition to being able to keep the security of your day job, independent inventing has some decent statistics to lean on. Of course, it's not a guaranteed road to riches but the odds are in your favor because keeping your day job means that you'll be able to survive until you profit from your independent creativity.

The self-proclaimed experts in the independent invention field are currently stating that you have a 10 times better chance of starting your own business and getting a product on the market than by trying to become an independent inventor. What they leave out is the failure rates for new businesses coupled with the 80 percent market failure of new products.

I'm going to take a different tact and recommend the licensing process because I've seen what licensing can do for inventors if you follow the rules properly.

Even though you probably won't find a formal set of written guidelines for most industries that are interested in new innovations from independent inventors, there are a few and the success that other inventors have had with the process gives us a pretty good idea of what's expected of independent inventors to achieve success in licensing.

Rather than randomly trying to exploit our products, logic dictates that if we create a new product for an industry that the successful firms in that industry would have a better idea of whether it would be successful or not. What's more, these successful firms are already established and have the channels of manufacturing and marketing already in place so why not offer them the opportunity to exploit the idea in return for a percentage of the sales?

Why not indeed? This is the licensing process and for all of it's pitfalls and uncertainties its made millionaires out of people who would have otherwise gone bankrupt attempting to do it all themselves.

Even though it's a statistical crapshoot and ends up being a combination of a numbers game coupled with timing, it's still one of the most lucrative ways to get your new ideas marketed and besides, the odds are better than the lottery.

To quote an industry that depends on it, consider that licensing is what most of the big name authors have done with their work. Statistically, successful authors who actually write books and then submit them to a publisher usually collect between 200 to 500 rejection slips before they get a publisher to sign a contract with them.

To license your inventions, you must make a working prototype to prove to a potential licensee that it works and does what you say it will do.

For example, would-be authors who write book proposals and outlines don't spend as much time writing as writers, but because they don't actually complete anything until they find an interested publisher, they only have about 20 percent of the success that authors who write first have.

This means that they have to submit between 1,000 and 2,500 proposals to find a publisher. The problem is that there aren't that many publishers available to them so the odds go even higher.

This directly correlates to inventors who have prototypes as opposed to those who have jotted down ideas. Companies who are interested in licensing new inventions are looking to the inventor to prove that the idea works. If the organization wanted unproven ideas, they'd probably do it in-house and maintain absolute control over the work that was being done.

Incidentally, the success of this process assumes that you, as an independent inventor, will ignore the *not invented here* mindset of some organizations and continue to look for companies that are open to looking at outside inventions.

There are no rules that say a firm, or an industry, has to look at outside inventions. It's a decision that each organization makes and the only way you'll know for sure is to ask them.

There are organizations like government agencies and educational institutions that regularly advertise for new inventions. The US Government's Small Business Innovative Research grant programs http://www.sba.gov/SBIR/indexsbir-sttr.html is an example of a two-billion dollar per year funding program for new ways to do things that the government has deemed important.

A few years ago, the University of Texas in Austin was posting their internal statistics and reported through the Office of Technology Licensing and Intellectual Property, that in 1998 to 2001, they received 253 disclosures and at the end of the year 2001, the 20 percent were in process (the rest were still sitting and waiting for their turn). They also reported that the inventors had been paid approximately $3 million in royalties over that period.

That's one in five that were funded for exploitation. Do these numbers sound familiar? So, what does all this mean to you, the independent inventor? If you review the options you have, you'll discover that you can:

1. Work for someone else and develop their ideas into marketable products.

2. Start and operate your own business.

3. Create innovative solutions and sell the rights to someone else.

Statistically, you've got a better chance for financial stability by working for someone else but you'll never get rich nor will you have the freedom to exploit your own individualism.

Starting your own business may be a viable option but it's a major life-changing decision and has the potential of making you very successful, becoming a way of life, or driving you to the poor house. It does, however, allow you the freedom to explore your options and exercise both your creativity and your business expertise.

Licensing is the middle ground in the creative process. It allows you the opportunity to exercise your creative talents, with minimal financial risk, and offers you the possibility of high profitability long after the creative work has been done.

If you look through all the possibilities and add up all the statistics you can find for licensing a new invention, you'll probably find that an independent inventor has about a one-half to a one-fourth percent chance of getting a new idea to market.

If those odds don't look too appealing, remember that your risk is minimal, the out of pocket investment you'll have to make to see if you've got the next great product is minor compared to doing it all yourself, and the potential, if your idea takes off, is huge.

I had the privilege of working with inventors who have gone on to make more money than I did with their innovations. I also worked with the companies who licensed the inventions and learned that there are ground rules to being successful, just like any other business.

As far as the process of licensing new inventions is concerned, I've personally been involved with a variety of licensed projects since the 1970's and the most successful was the Teddy Ruxpin project in the 1980's. You can read the TRUE story of how it all happened at http://www.mindspring.com/~mathue/faq3.html. This non-patented product made the inventors over $80 million in royalties.

Another example is when I did consulting work for Coleco Toys. While I was consulting for them, they licensed the Cabbage Patch Kids from an inventor named Xavier Roberts and turned the line into a $600 million per year endeavor.

When you consider that Coleco Toys was doing $1.2 billion in business, the Cabbage Patch Kids represented 50 percent of their gross revenue and Xavier got a percentage of everything connected with the sale of the Cabbage Patch Kids line. Not too bad, for an ugly little doll with yarn hair, was it?

What made the Cabbage Patch Kids unique were their birth certificate and adoption papers—not the doll itself. The doll, by anybody's assessment was ugly but because it gave the little girl the opportunity to adopt, name, and receive a birthday card for her own baby doll, the product was unique and became a billion dollar runaway hit.

Notice that what made the doll so popular was neither complicated nor expensive to produce (a couple of pieces of paper and some (postage) but it was unique enough to capture the attention and the pocketbooks of the public.

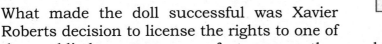

What made the doll successful was Xavier Roberts decision to license the rights to one of the world's largest toy manufacturers so they could exploit it to its fullest, something that Xavier realized he wasn't capable or interested in doing.

As you consider licensing, always keep in mind that:

1. NOT all the simple things have been invented and

2. NOT all the needs of the world have been addressed.

Chapter 2
Tips For Inventors

Even if you decide to do nothing after you read *How to Sell Your Inventions for Cash,* you'll get an insight and an education about what goes on when you read about some kid who got rich and bought a new Jaguar for cash, but was not old enough to drive it.

Although every inventor is creative, not every creative idea gets to market even if you decide to license it. It's a long step from inventing to licensing your invention. Many inventors stop because they don't have the money to create a prototype or are afraid that someone, someplace, will rip them off.

Investigating the licensing of your invention is a logical process, which you can accomplish in about eight weeks, for about $1,000. *How to Sell Your Inventions for Cash* will take you through the process, step by step, to find a licensee (buyer) for your invention. When you've completed the solicitation and market research process, you'll know if you've got the next hit or whether you should table this invention and move on to something else.

No matter what you invent you'll be able to use this tried-and-true solicitation and market research process. The approach is based on a logical, mechanical, marketing research process and works 100 percent of the time. Bear in mind, however, that you might not like the results you get because the process might tell you that your idea is not currently marketable.

There are many things to consider when embarking on the licensing process but rather than clutter up your life with all of them, we've refined them down into a handful of ideas and suggestions that virtually all inventors will find useful and productive.

The Fundamental Aspects of Licensing

As you proceed, keep the following items in mind at all times:

- To license your idea you must have a prototype. This is part of your responsibility, not the licensee.

- Have a novelty search conducted by a patent attorney if your item is patentable. This is NOT to encourage you to get a patent. It is to prevent you from unknowingly violating someone else's patent.

- Even if you decide that a patent is warranted, use the one-year window of marketing research to find a buyer for your invention before spending the big dollars on the patenting process.

Going Public

Inventors are concerned about publicizing their invention for fear of having it stolen or exploited by others.

In the world of marketing, advertising is creating the awareness that something exists. A sale is the only reason to advertise because if you don't tell, you can't sell. Licensing is a form of marketing. If you're going to find someone to license your invention, you're going to have to start telling people about it and this means going public with your invention.

There has been some confusion about what going public means. Fortunately, the USPTO has provided us with a wonderful definition that actually forms the basis for the patent process. What they say is that going public is when any one of these occurrences takes place:

1. Advertising the invention publicly, or

2. Offering the invention for sale (making a solicitation and market research process), or

3. Describing the invention in a private or public publication.

After publicly disclosing a conceivably patentable idea, if the inventor doesn't file for a patent within one-year, the idea becomes public domain. What this means to you, the inventor, is that you've got a one-year window to test your invention for marketability or in this case, licensing potential.

If during the one-year period you discover that you've got a marketable or licensable item, you might want to consider patenting it. (See the section on patents before you decide to get one.)

If, on the other hand, you discover that your invention isn't currently marketable, don't bother to get a patent because that won't change the marketability and will just end up costing you money.

Public Domain

Public domain refers to the status of a work having no protection and, therefore, belonging to the world. When a work is *in* or has *fallen into* public domain, it means it is available for unrestricted use by anyone. Permission and/or payment are not required to use public domain material. These include originally non-copyrightable or non-patentable items, lost copyrights, expired patents and copyrights, and government documents.

No Bad Ideas

If your idea works, it's a good idea. Marketing appeal is another story. Most uninformed people judge whether an invention is good based on whether it achieves mass manufacturing and distribution. Certainly, this is a judgment for profitability but it has little, if anything, to do with value.

Industrial engineers create one-of-a-kind tooling that keeps hundreds, perhaps thousands, of people employed for years, and yet when the product line is phased out, the tooling is scrapped. Nobody would contest the value of that single invention called production tooling, yet only one unit of production tooling was ever produced. Since it worked, it was a good idea but it was not mass marketed.

Don't be discouraged by the lack of success or understanding that other people exhibit. Unless their judgment directly affects your ability to creatively invent or make money with your idea it's not important.

Timing

We're living in a world that is technologically reinventing itself every one to five years. If you question this statistic, look at the changes in the world of products, services, teaching methods, and job requirements that have significantly changed in your lifetime.

Look at the following examples and think about what's happened to these products that you have purchased:

- Automotive technology—the latest innovations and accessories are upgraded or replaced within five years from their introduction. Fuel cell cars and the electric vehicles were a designers dream a few years ago.

- Cellular telephone technology lasts for about 12 months or until another significant improvement gives us a reason to buy new equipment. The latest versions incorporate wireless e-mail, video transmission, calendaring, scheduling, and color.

- Audio products are lasting less than one year and the new solid-state technologies are shortening that cycle as well. CD audio players are available for less than $20 and MP3 players that fit in a shirt pocket and play over 12 hours of material are below $50.

- Personal computer technology is changing at a pace of every six to twelve months and even a shorter time cycle when you include all the accessories. Pocket computers or personal digital assistants (PDA's) like the $100 Palm Pilot and related units are becoming more powerful and are being upgraded twice a year.

- Pocket size video systems and digital cameras have given new meaning to the world of photography with newer, more powerful, and more affordable equipment becoming available every year. The ability to edit and process video in a laptop computer is a common configuration. Digital cameras have marked the demise of Polaroid because we can now instantly capture, view and print images.

- The fashion industry has had five buying seasons for over thirty years: spring, summer, winter, fall, and Christmas. What's next—Easter and back to school?

- Software borders on obsolescence when it's released. The proliferation of the software has allowed developers to implement significant changes that warrant obsoleting the existing version and offering a newer version with improved capabilities.

- Gadgets to make our lives simpler and easier to handle abound by the bucketsful. Just take a trip to Wal-Mart, Pep Boys, or the local cooking store and look at all the wonderful goodies and inventions that were not there last month, that are there this month and will probably be gone next month.

- I spent years in the toy and game industry. We felt we were lucky if a product lasted for a full year and if it held on for two or three years, it became a staple and we'd all look forward to big Christmas bonuses.

What does this mean to you as an inventor? It means that the world is moving fast and creating lots of opportunities for innovative people like you to conceive, develop, and offer your ideas to the world.

It also means that the window of opportunity may open and close before you're ready. The day has passed when an inventor can retreat to his or her workshop and release their ideas when they think they're ready.

The world may pass you by while you were working on the idea. What's even worse is when you procrastinate because you're not quite ready to do something. Chances are, someone else is ready and they'll beat you to the marketplace.

It makes no difference whether you miss the opportunity by days or years— you've still missed it.

To ensure that you don't miss this window of opportunity, it's critical that you be reading and reviewing at least three trade journals on a monthly basis that serve that industry. This research will tell you what's hot, what's not, what's wanted, what's needed, how fast the trends are maturing and just how long trends last before they're improved or replaced.

Here's a note of consideration—patenting. Since patenting always seems to enter into the discussions about the success of innovations and inventions, a serious consideration is that since the marketability of an item is the prime consideration here, it is crucial to assess the value of whether or not a patent will be of assistance in the sale of an item. Patenting takes an inordinate amount of time and the delays in obtaining patent status might prevent the innovation from getting to the market in time to be profitable.

Targeting Needs of Others

Inventing things for your own personal needs or interests can be entertaining and fulfilling, but it's seldom profitable. To be financially successful, you must invent for the needs of others.

The financial success of your inventiveness has two basic marketing methodologies: product push and market pull.

Product push or pioneering is when the inventor develops a product to solve a problem or addresses something that is not needed and necessary. The public has to be educated about the product, services, benefits, uses, and convinced of all the wonderful reasons why this invention will make them money, save them money, save them time, or make things easier for them.

When you develop an answer, where there is not a clear question in the minds of the public, like "when is somebody going to build a better something or other," the public must be educated to the benefits of your inventiveness and agree with them before they will spend their money.

Although many new products are marketed this way, it's an expensive and somewhat uncertain method of entering the marketplace regardless of how useful or innovative your idea may be. Product push carries a high degree of risk because the public may never be educated to the point where they appreciate the value of the invention and consequently never purchase enough to make it a financial success.

The alternative is to invent for the needs of others or to address concerns that have already been defined and where the buyer will pay for the solution.

This is commonly called market pull or find a need and fill it. It's easier (and far more profitable) because the buyer has already defined a need. You're filling that need with a better product or service.

The most common example is when bidding on a government requirement like SBIR Grants (Small Business Innovative Research). An agency of the federal government, like the Department of Defense, defines a specific need and allocates up to $100,000 for a paper solution to the problem and up to $750,000 to build a prototype and prove that the concept that was defined on paper actually works.

Although your solution to the problem may be unique and proprietarily yours, there is already a pot of gold at the end of the rainbow because the government has announced publicly that they will pay for a viable solution.

This defines your responsibility as an inventor as having to create a viable solution to their problem and relieves you of the pressure of having to find a market. The government is the market and the one who pays the bills.

This is the prime reason that people and companies prefer to do business with the government—they fit the two rules for financially successful inventing, which are:

Rule #1: Follow the money.

Rule #2: See rule #1. If there's no dough there, don't go there, period!

Even though working with the government can be tedious and frustrating, there's a 99.999 percent assurance that the money is there and that if we create a product or service that fills their needs that we'll be paid.

Prototype

Your idea should have at least one prototype that works. Although it's not impossible to sell an idea or invention without a working model or prototype, it's very difficult.

Merriam-Webster defines a prototype as a first full-scale and usually functional form of a new type or design of a construction.

The concept of licensing your invention is based on a proven invention that works. This requires the embodiment of the idea or the building of a working model to prove to the potential licensee that it's not only a good invention, but that you know how to make it work, at least in a preliminary form.

The basic ground rules for creating prototypes are as follows:

1. If your innovation is based on the way something works, it must work properly.

2. If your idea is based on appearance, then it must look good.

3. If it is based on both, then you must do your best to combine functionality and appearance into the same model without seriously compromising either one.

If you're not capable of creating your own prototype, you'll need to contract with someone to turn your ideas and inventions into a physical example so that the potential licensees won't have to use their imagination. The more you ask a potential licensee to use their imagination about how your invention looks and operates, the greater the likelihood that they will misunderstand it completely and reject the idea.

The materials you use for your prototype should be as consistent as possible with the production unit. Of course, since this is a prototype, a degree of flexibility is allowed especially if the manufacturer understands the nature of the production materials and processes.

Sometimes, a paper prototype works best. Many preliminary mockups are done with paper and work as well as any other material. If you combine the paper mockup with a carefully crafted video demonstration where the person handling the prototype is careful, you might be able to convince the viewer that the person is handling a production unit.

Paper Model of Select a Game

When I was in the toy business, the stage after a drawing was a heavy paper mockup that was colored, decorated as close as possible, to the size, shape, and configuration of the finished toy.

The Internet

With the maturation of the Internet (net) and the World Wide Web (web) into viable business tools, the serious inventor has tools that are unsurpassed in their ease of use and return on investment.

The different tools of the Internet lend themselves to all aspects of the invention process but not all the time. Examine the tools carefully and then decide which tool is appropriate for your particular needs.

Functionally, the net is a lot of computers that can talk to each other through the phone, cable, and satellite systems of the world. The web is similar to a gigantic library within the Internet, and it's generally accessible by anyone who has access to the Internet.

Since the web is a gigantic library of text and multimedia content, a web site, known as a universal resource locator (URL), is the electronic equivalent of a book, catalog, or other information storage medium.

The most powerful component of the web is its ability to hyperlink, hot link, or more simply, jump from one location to another with the simple click of a mouse button. This point and click capability continually expands the capabilities of the web and makes it a powerful tool for the inventor looking for information and guidance.

Resources for Inventors

The invention process can be both taxing and draining on your time and financial resources. To help save you time and money in your efforts, we've included some proven sources of help to help ensure your success.

Schools

If you're looking for quality assistance that is reasonably priced, seriously consider contacting the high schools, colleges, universities, and trade schools. These facilities can provide you with low-cost assistance (intern programs) in completing your prototype, rather than turning to expensive professional prototype development firms for the work. They're called intern programs.

Schools have talented students who can assist you for a fraction of the cost of professional prototype development firms. Be sure to use nondisclosure forms when you are discussing matters with them and ALWAYS use a Work-for-hire Agreement when you have anybody work on your invention. This insures that whatever work or research they do on the project or product belongs to you and not to them.

Students can often provide first-class services at reasonable prices for things like:

- Prototypes and graphic arts. If you can't create your own prototype, consider using students who are majoring in the type of skill that you need to get a first-class prototype built for you. Give them a little latitude and capitalize on their creative genius as a part of the work. After all, this is what they're going to do for their career and it could benefit you to allow them to add a little of what they have to offer to your product.

- Photography and videotaping. At some juncture, you're going to need photographs and perhaps, even a video demonstration tape to clone your prototype and to use as an advertising and promotion tool.

There are students who are majoring in photography, videography, editing, advertising, and a variety of related majors that require that they not only become proficient at their craft, but that they obtain cash assignments while they are in school. Speak with the teachers and ask them to recommend students for the tasks you require.

- Composition and written copy. Like it or not, your work to poll and solicit the marketplace for your ideas and innovations is going to require advertising style writing skills. Even if you find advertising rhetoric a waste of time, the people who are reading your creativity do not. Students who are majoring in advertising, creative writing, and marketing are logical candidates to hire as copywriters for your advertising and promotional brochures.

You can supply the technological inputs, operational characteristics, and mechanical specifications, but you are better served to let someone who writes creative advertising copy wordsmith the information into an acceptable format that will pique the curiosity of the potential licensee to the point where they pick up the phone and call you for more detailed information.

- Telephone follow-up. The process that we're describing in *How to Sell Your Inventions for Cash* relies on a series of events taking place to make sure that no stone is left unturned. Part of the process involves calling the people who have been sent your materials and asking them for their opinion. This is simple but it is NOT easy. Statistically, you are going to get more people who do NOT like your idea than those that do.

  Creative individuals are protective and defensive about their creations (sort of like a baby) and when someone on the other end of the phone rejects the concept, we tend to take it personally. This rejection factor builds up until we stop doing our follow-up calls which marks the end of the project, whether we have found a buyer or not.

  Hire speech, drama, marketing, or just vocally gifted students to make the initial telephone follow up. When they locate the individuals who have a genuine interest in your new inventions, you call them. Leave the rejection to someone who is getting paid to put up with it and who does not have a vested interest in the idea.

Libraries

One of the most frequently overlooked resources, and still one of the most valuable, is the public library, more specifically, the reference section and the reference librarians.

You'll need trade journals and reference items that are available at the library. The reference librarians, most of who have master's degree in Library Science and who are experts at locating things, will be thrilled to help you locate any information.

For example, you should subscribe to and read, each month, at least three trade journals that service the industry in which you've decided to invent. Before you run out and subscribe to these publications, go to the library and sample several of them before making a decision to pay for copies that you might not utilize.

The Golden Rule

The one with the gold makes the rules. Every industry has its rules, and every manufacturer within that industry has its rules as well. Since you're going to be asking companies to buy what it is that you're selling, they have the gold, so they get to make the rules.

One of the chief objections that manufacturers have in doing business with outside inventors is that the inventors don't know about, or sometimes don't even care about, the specific industry rules that govern that industry.

Even though an invention appears to be a good idea, the inventor may not have taken into consideration industry rules or regulations and therefore doomed the product to failure before it even gets started.

Every inventor's responsibilities include knowing and, to the greatest extent practicable, complying with the industry rules and regulations for maximum acceptance of their inventions.

The industry rules can usually be found by contacting the editors of the major trade journals for that industry in which you have chosen to invent. These publications tend to be the guardians and watchdogs of the industry. They're usually knowledgeable about where you can obtain the latest rules, regulations, codes of compliance, and other applicable documents to help ensure that what you do complies with the latest standards.

Reasons Inventors Fail

We need to review the five primary reasons why independent inventors fail to make money with their ideas and inventions. I'll bet you didn't want to hear this part, did you?

In order to be successful you need to know all the pitfalls and problems so you can avoid them. I'm going to remind you once again that if the idea works, it's a great idea. What we're concerned with is the marketability and more specifically, the profitability.

The five statements below should be committed to memory, taped to your mirror, glued to the outside of your purse, and sewn to your Fruit of the Loom's. They comprise 98 percent of the reasons why your great ideas won't make you any money:

1. The invention is more complex than the problem merits.

2. The invention isn't new.

3. You haven't fully considered the problem.

4. No one wants it.

5. You've got an unrealistic idea of the value of your invention.

As you create new ideas and inventions, look closely at these five simple concepts and see if you're guilty of violating one or more of them. If you were, I'd recommend that you make some changes quickly.
જ

Chapter 3
Cover Your Assets

Virtually every creative individual I've ever met is concerned about somebody, somewhere, stealing their original ideas and exploiting them without giving them their fair due. While this might be a valid concern, it isn't always the case and should not become the primary focus that decides whether to exploit your creativity.

My logic comes from the fact that I've yet to meet an independent inventor in one of my seminars over the past 20 years who has personally, or knows someone personally, who has divulged their invention to someone and had it ripped-off and taken to market.

I'm not saying that it doesn't happen because it does. What I am saying is that the incidence of it happening is so small that it's of little concern or consequence to you.

Nevertheless, there are aspects of the legal system that must, out of the necessity of our society and business dealings, be considered and applied to the independent invention process to ensure that you are operating within the guidelines of today's business world. The process of protecting your original work and legally protecting it under the law is called intellectual property law.

First and foremost, the law does NOT elicit compliance—respect for the law does. The fact that you have taken all of the proper steps to secure the legal rights to your ideas, innovations, and creations does not mean that someone will not attempt to exploit them without your permission and without compensating you.

The laws are not physically prohibitive, but they do allow for recourse in the event that you believe that you or your creativity have been unfairly utilized or exploited. This is the reason for establishing the ownership claims for yourself and your inventions.

Next, let's define what we mean by intellectual property. By strict definition, intellectual property is a trade secret, patent, trademark, service mark or copyright. The process for legally securing the rights to your intellectual property varies with the type and style of the property and the manner under which you will be working with it.

Currently, there are three aspects to the laws governing intellectual property:

1. Date of discovery documentation: poor man's patent, Provisional patent and inventor's notebooks.

2. Contractual documentation: nondisclosure agreement, invention nonuse agreement, Work-for-hire Agreement, contingent commitment agreement and licensing agreements.

3. Federal registration: patenting (full patent), trademark and copyright

What we need to do now is define and examine each of these three aspects to determine which, if any, of them are appropriate for your needs and if they are, how to properly and expeditiously obtain and utilize them.

Trade Secret

Trade secret is a legal term referring to any information, whether or not copyrightable or patentable, including formulas, patterns, compilations, programs, methods, techniques and processes, and business information, that derives independent economic value, actual or potential, from not being generally known to, and not being readily ascertainable by proper means by other persons who can obtain economic value from its disclosure or use, and is the subject of efforts that are reasonable under the circumstances to maintain its secrecy.

Know-how has no legal definition. Usually it refers to one of two situations: confidential know-how which is equivalent to trade secrets, and non-confidential know-how, which is readily discoverable by reverse engineering, or is information generally known in the trade.

A third definition of know-how is any information needed to run a business such as how to market a product. Because of these varying definitions, know-how needs to be specifically defined either in a licensing agreement or by implication through the manner in which it is used.

Usually it is better to use the term trade secret instead of know-how when information is not generally available.

Tangible research property (TRP) means tangible (or corporeal) items produced in the course of research projects. TRP is separate and distinct from intangible (or intellectual) property such as inventions, patents, trademarks, trade secrets, copyrights, etc. Individual items of TRP may be associated with one or more intangible properties such as patents or copyrights. TRP includes such items as:

- biological materials
- computer software
- computer databases
- prototype devices

- engineering drawings
- integrated circuit chips
- circuit diagrams
- equipment

Property means intellectual property and tangible research property.

Let's start with the basics: How do you keep a secret a secret? Simple: you don't tell anyone. That's the long and the short of trade secret agreements. There are situations where you don't want anyone to know certain things about your invention. Period!

The value of this statement and the concept of trade secrets is available to inventors but of questionable value since in order to license the invention, you'll probably have to disclose everything sooner or later.

Nevertheless, during the development phase of your invention and perhaps even after it has been sold or licensed, trade secret may be an integral requirement for profitable exploitation of the innovation.

Popular examples of the trade secret process are the formula for Coca Cola and the process for hardening certain metals to industrial strengths. Coke has never divulged their recipe and remains in a locked vault. It's secrecy has never prevented the soft drink from being enjoyed nor has it been a detriment to the money making power of the invention.

We utilize metals every day in airplanes and other vehicles that have been hardened and strengthened through secret processes known only to their manufacturers. Notice that even though we don't understand how the result came to be, we still benefit from the process that was used to create the alloy.

During the development of your inventions, keeping your idea as secret as possible will probably be a good idea since global communications, and especially the Internet, has made it possible to disseminate new information globally at the speed of light.

In today's rapidly changing world, being able to keep your secrets proprietary a little longer than the competition could make the difference between being the primary product to hit the retail shelves or another knock off of an innovative product.

Requiring that employees, subcontractors, and suppliers sign a trade secret agreement is not considered unduly restrictive nor is it an uncommon practice where the proprietary nature of your work is concerned.

Description of Trade Secret Reminder

The Trade Secret Reminder contains the following items:

AA: Date of the agreement (day, month and year i.e. 21st of May, 2020).

BB: Person or organization that is agreeing to receive the information.

CC: Person or organization that is offering to divulge the information.

DD: A full description of the relative merits and/or benefits of the idea or innovation including any sub-points.

Trade Secret Reminder

```
   Date:  AA
     To:  BB
   From:  CC
Subject:  Trade Secrets Reminder
```

The items described below belong to CC.

They are considered trade secrets and information regarding these items is not to be divulged or used by parties who have not received written authorization from the owner!

This is to remind you of CC's position regarding the trade secret status of the following items: DD.

CC owns all rights, including trade secret rights in the above listed items. This means that you may not legally divulge or discuss the items with third parties without my written permission. This obligation to keep the items confidential will continue to exist even if you are no longer connected with CC.

Please don't hesitate to ask any questions you might have regarding trade secrets, ownership rights, or anything else related to this subject. If you have no questions, please sign the acknowledgment at the bottom of this letter and return it to me, keeping a copy for your own records.

Thank you for your cooperation.

ACKNOWLEDGMENT

I have read and agree to be bound by the statements in the above memo.

_____

BB Signature   Date

Date of Discovery Documentation

Date of discovery documents prove that on a certain date you discovered, developed, or otherwise created certain specific ideas, inventions or innovations.

The most important aspect of all discovery documents is that by themselves, they have NO validity or value in any kind of legal proceedings. They establish a date of discovery. To be of any value, they MUST be used in conjunction with another legal document such as a patent.

Poor Man's Patent

This simple document was made famous by Alexander Graham Bell when he used it in the Patent Court of Appeals to prove that he had actually conceived the notion of the undulating current, the principle by which the telephone works, prior to the date claimed by a French inventor named Gray.

The Patent Court of Appeals required that both parties in the action submit written proof of their earliest date of conception of the idea for the telephone.

Because Bell was too poor during his inventing days to afford separate writing paper, he wrote a letter to his intended bride on the back of a piece of butcher paper that he had used to sketch his concept for the telephone. Since the letter was dated and mailed to his fiancée, the date of the postmark was considered as a valid date and having bled through the paper, the date was considered valid for the design on the back of the paper as well.

Bell's letter predated Gray's documentation and the rights to the telephone were awarded to Bell. This story can be found in video called *The Story of Alexander Graham Bell* starring Don Ameche.

Because of the notoriety of the case and the wide acceptance of the telephone in the years following the court case, many inventors have decided to send themselves registered letters mistakenly believing that the letter alone would serve as all the protection they needed for their creative genius.

The reality of the process shows us that it was a dated document that proved a date of discovery and was used in conjunction with a patent application. Without the patent application, the letter would have proved meaningless.

All negative aspects aside, the process of *date stamping* new innovations may prove to be a useful tool in a patent lawsuit. With more organizations rewarding employees for initiative and creativity, the process will be more likely to be useful in resolving industry or corporate arguments.

The procedure for using a Poor Man's Patent, is as follows:

1. Place all of the pertinent data and documentation regarding your innovation in an envelope.

2. ALL the flaps and openings MUST be sealed with paper tape (no tape plastic allowed). This is to insure the integrity of the seal and only paper allows signatures to be affixed to the taped openings.

3. Mail the envelope to yourself via Registered Mail.

4. When you receive the envelope, label the exterior of the package so that you know what's inside.

5. Place the sealed envelope in a safe place (like a safety deposit box or locked file).

6. If you ever need to open the envelope to prove your date of discovery, seriously consider videotaping the event in front of a judge to guarantee that the integrity of the process is NOT compromised.

Notary

Under NO CIRCUMSTANCES should you use a notary public for the date verification process! Notarization does not guarantee the truth or accuracy of statements in a document. The Notary has no obligation to verify a document's contents. Notarization does **not** legalize or validate a document. Notarization establishes the authenticity of the signer and the date of signing.

Provisional Patent

Under US Patent law, the first-to-invent gets the patent rights. However, this only applies if you can prove you were the first person to come up with the idea.

Mailing yourself a letter with your invention notes will not necessarily prove your conception date for the patent office. They recommend that you keep a detailed log book which describes the activities you took to create and test the invention.

Even with a log book, it is often difficult to prove you came up with an invention before someone else. That's why the first person to file a patent application is almost always deemed to be the first to invent, and why provisional patents have become so popular—because they establish an official US Patent filing date for the date that the invention was first reduced to practice.

A provisional patent was designed to solve an age-old problem. You want to see if your invention has commercial appeal, but if you tell people, you run the risk they will steal the idea. Non-disclosure agreements can help, but not everyone is willing to sign one.

The solution was the Provisional Patent Application which lets you quickly secure an initial filing date for your invention and legally allows you to use the words patent pending.

Once a provisional patent application is filed, you have 12 months to test your idea and seek funding before filing a full patent application. If you choose to file the full patent before the end of the 12-month period, the filing date can relate back to the date you filed your provisional patent application.

If you decide not to move forward with your patent, then you can simply abandon it, knowing your upfront costs were minimal.

Filing a provisional patent application allows an inventor to claim patent pending status for the invention but involves only a small fraction of the work and cost of a patent application. All that is required to file a provisional patent application is a $80 fee ($160 for large inventors) and:

1. Informal drawing(s), if needed to understand how to make and use the invention.

2. A one-page cover sheet.

3. An appropriate small entity declaration(s) if you are seeking small entity status.

The detailed description of the invention can even be a technical paper you have written for a journal, if the paper meets the legal standards for describing how to make and use the invention. This allows an inventor to freely publish an invention without fear of losing potential patent rights.

The USPTO doesn't examine a provisional patent application when it is filed. If you file a patent application within one-year and claim the provisional patent application's filing date, the provisional patent application will be examined.

The provisional patent must have fully described the structure and operation of the invention being claimed in the patent application.

NOTE: Your patent application may not include any new matter (technical information) that wasn't in the provisional patent application.

There are several advantages of filing a provisional patent application:

Lower cost and faster preliminary process—The provisional patent filing fee is much less expensive than a full patent fee. In addition, the technical requirements are simplified, which means it takes much less time and money to prepare and file a provisional patent application.

Establishes an official US patent filing date—Full patent applications filed within twelve months of the provisional application date have the benefit of "relating back" to the provisional patent application.

One year to assess the commercial viability of your invention—You can take advantage of the provisional patent's one-year pendency period to evaluate the commercial potential of your invention before committing to the upfront costs of obtaining a full patent. If you decide to make modifications to your invention during the one-year period, you can file a new provisional patent application and then consolidate both provisional patents into one regular patent.

Use of the patent pending notice—Prior to the advent of the provisional patent application, an inventor had to file a full patent application in order to use the label "patent pending" or "patent applied for." You may now do so upon filing a provisional patent application.

Extending the patent term—A patent lasts for 20 years, measured from the date that a full patent application is filed. By first filing a provisional patent that lasts for 12 months, you could conceivably extend your patent rights by a full year.

Confidentiality—A provisional patent preserves the confidentiality of your application without publication.

As of the date of publication of this manuals, the fees are $200 to file or $100 for a small entity. Complete information about the Provisional Patent including downloadable forms and all the latest updates and fee schedules may be obtained at www.USPTO.gov.

Inventor's Notebooks

Of significance to industrial concerns, design groups, and individuals who are required to submit proof of discovery or who must show a significant sequence of events in the development of an idea for some form of legal or business purpose, an inventor's notebook may prove to be useful.

These notebooks are specially designed and fabricated to prevent cheating on the design process. Each page is actually two identically numbered pages with carbon paper. (That's right gang, real old-fashioned carbon paper.) The pages are stitched into the binding to prevent removal without destroying the pages and the numbering integrity of the entire notebook. They should be used with a pencil or ballpoint pen.

Many of the books also have a place on the bottom where you initial and date each page and have a witness sign and date them as well.

When there is a question within an organization regarding discovery dates, the innovator of an idea, the steps involved in a process, test results and dates, or other pertinent information that needs to be of a certifiable and traceable nature, the notebooks become an invaluable resource.

You can obtain them from a variety of sources including the bookstore at http://www.nolo.com.

The Value of Date of Discovery

Although each of the date stamp processes described establishes a date of discovery, by themselves they have no strength in the courts without being used as relevant information in support of some other form of protection where the date of discovery becomes an integral part of legally binding arbitration. They are currently important in four areas:

1. The establishment of the date of discovery in a patent application wherein two or more individuals are applying for a patent on similar or identical items. In this instance, the date of discovery may weigh heavily in determining which party is awarded the patent.

2. In civil lawsuits against employees that during their tenure of employment or following their employment with a firm, divulge the results of work that they developed to another firm or individual.

3. In the solicitation and market research package, when a manufacturer rejects your invention, and then produces the identical product. In this situation, unless the manufacturer can prove a prior date of discovery to the one shown in your documentation it may be possible to prove that they stole your invention.

4. The ability to establish a date of discovery in the development of the invention may become a focal point for prosecution of an individual for violation of trade secrets, company confidential information, and similar related situations.

Chapter 4
Contractual Documents

Because the ultimate objective of the creative process (at least as far as we're concerned) is to exploit your invention and make it a profitable enterprise, the majority of the documentation and related legal maneuvering covers new ideas, innovations, and inventions that are covered under contract law.

Six primary contractual documents are used with the invention process. They are: confidentiality or nondisclosure agreement, invention nonuse agreement, work-for-hire agreement, non-competition agreement, contingent commitment agreement, and licensing agreement. As an independent inventor, you should become familiar with and utilize them whenever possible to assist in the prevention of being unprofitably exploited.

I highly recommend that if you are unsure of the content, conditions, responsibilities, and recourse stated or implied in these documents that you seek the counsel of someone who is schooled in this element of the law and in whom you can and will place your trust.

Please note that although an attorney originally did the bulk of the work on these agreements, they may or may not be exactly what you want or need for your specific situation.

The first five of these documents are to be used when you are dealing with employees, vendors, subcontractors, or anyone with whom you discuss your invention prior to going public with the idea. The fifth is the licensing agreement itself, which will be covered in detail.

The objective of these documents is to establish an atmosphere of mutual understanding between the inventor and the person who is supplying services or information as to exactly what is confidential information, who owns it, and what level of disclosure constitutes a violation of that confidentiality.

Confidentiality or Nondisclosure

This fundamental document is used to bind an individual or an organization to confidentiality during the development cycle of an invention.

This is a legally binding, legally executable, legally prosecutable document in a court of law and can be used as the foundation for recovering monetary compensation if it can be proven that the recipient of the confidential information caused irreparable financial losses to the individual owning the rights to the proprietary information by the premature disclosure of the information.

A nondisclosure agreement's usage is generally misunderstood because inventors want to keep his or her ideas confidential and assume that everyone will be willing to sign the agreement. This is not the case. This is a prime example of the golden rule: the person with the gold gets to make the rules.

At this stage of your development process, where you are investing in the development of your invention and paying others to assist you, you get to make the rule, which is: "If you want to do business with me and get paid, you MUST sign the nondisclosure agreement. Period!"

Because you are in control of the money, the other party must comply with your rule or they don't get to participate. However, make note of the following regarding this agreement:

- Many potential suppliers and subcontractors will not sign the agreement because they don't want to be bothered with worrying about what's confidential and what's not.

- If confidentiality is critical to your development, do NOT conduct business with people who will not sign this agreement.

- If the confidentiality is desirable but not a requirement, don't worry about it.

- Just because someone signs the nondisclosure agreement, don't assume that they won't divulge the information anyway. The agreement gives you recourse if they do divulge but it carries no guarantees that the information will not be passed on to someone else.

The opposite of this situation is when you, as the inventor, try to force a potential licensee to sign a nondisclosure agreement. Since they are now in control of the money, they get to decide whether or not they want to sign the agreement and in most situations, they will not sign it because they do not want to commit to anything until they know exactly what is involved.

The basic nondisclosure agreement asserts the following items:

- The information you are about to divulge is truly proprietary and confidential.

- The information was developed by you and is yours to use, divulge, or generally make decisions about.

- The recipient of the information agrees to keep the information in confidence for as long as it remains confidential.

Although nondisclosure agreements create a sense of security for inventors, when organizations and individuals refuse to sign and abide by the tenants of the agreement, the inventor usually starts to become concerned that the other party is trying to rip them off and retreats to a position of extreme paranoia and caution.

Although the natural human tendency is to immediately distrust the other party due to their unwillingness to sign the agreement, the business climate and the standard operating rules for their industry will probably have far more to do with their reluctance to sign the agreement than any thoughts about impropriety or the theft of your intellectual property.

Assess each situation independently and decide for yourself whether the signing, of lack of signing, of the nondisclosure agreement is a necessary component of the successful exploitation of your invention or something that would be nice to have.

Description of Nondisclosure Agreement

The Nondisclosure Agreement contains the following items:

AA: Person or organization that is offering to divulge the information.

BB: Person or organization that is agreeing to receive the information.

Nondisclosure Agreement

Agreement and acknowledgment between AA and BB.

Whereas, AA agrees to furnish BB certain confidential information relating to the affairs of AA for purposes of review, revision, negotiation, and/or potential mutual business dealings, and

Whereas, BB agrees to review, examine, inspect or obtain such information only for the purposes described above, and to otherwise hold such information confidential pursuant to the terms of this agreement,

Be it known, that AA has or shall furnish to BB certain confidential information, and may further allow BB the right to inspect the business of AA and/or interview employees or representatives of AA, all on the following conditions:

1.   BB agrees to hold all confidential or proprietary information or trade secrets (information) in trust and confidence and agrees that it shall be used only for the contemplated purpose, and shall not be used for any other purpose or disclosed to any third party.

2.   No copies will be made or retained of any written information supplied, other than for the specific and exclusive usage in conjunction with AA's project.

3.   At the conclusion of negotiations, or upon demand by AA, all information, including written notes, photographs, memoranda, or notes taken by BB may be requested to be returned to AA.

4.   This information shall not be disclosed to any employee or consultant unless they agree to execute and be bound by the terms of this agreement.

5.   It is understood that BB shall have no obligation with respect to any information known by BB or generally known within the industry prior to date of this agreement, or which becomes common knowledge within the industry thereafter.

_____

CC Signature   Date

_____

DD Signature   Date

Invention Nonuse

The invention nonuse carries the same basic tenants as the nondisclosure agreement but the primary difference is that the nondisclosure agreement is generic in nature and covers anything that is discussed or disclosed during a meeting. An invention nonuse agreement specifically describes or calls out a particular device or process that is under consideration. The document may go into specific detail about what is allowed, not allowed, what's confidential and proprietary and what isn't.

Because discussion during the preliminary development stages of an idea tends to wander from the original concept into ancillary areas, invention nonuse is not recommended when you do NOT have a physical prototype or where general discussion might ensue.

Where it is useful and valuable is when you are working with a physical sample of an idea and need to present it to a developer, tester, or analyst and you want to bind them to strict confidentiality about this item alone.

Description of Invention Nonuse Agreement

The Invention Nonuse Agreement contains the following items:

AA: Date of the agreement (day, month and year i.e. 21st of May, 2005).

BB: Person or organization that is offering to divulge the information.

CC: Is the shortened name of BB.

DD: Person or organization that is agreeing to receive the information.

EE: Is the shortened name of CC.

FF: A signature of an independent, disinterested, third party who will attest, by signing the document, to the veracity of the statements contained in the document including the willingness of the parties involved to sign the document without coercion.

GG: A full description of the relative merits and/or benefits of the idea or innovation including any sub-points.

HH: State in which the agreement is signed.

II: County in which the agreement is signed.

Invention Nonuse Agreement

THIS AGREEMENT is made and entered into this AA day of AA, AA, by and between BB, hereinafter referred to as the CC, and DD, hereinafter referred to as the EE.

WITNESSETH: FF

WHEREAS, CC represents that it has invented a device, which is designed for the purpose of GG and,

WHEREAS, EE desires to evaluate the commercial utility of the invention before entering into an agreement with CC and,

WHEREAS, CC desires to keep its invention confidential in the event that EE, upon evaluation of the invention, does not desire to enter into an agreement with CC.

NOW, THEREFORE, in consideration of the premises and the mutual promises of the parties hereto, the parties agree as follows:

1.   Recitals. The above recitals are true.

2.   Disclosure. During the next 30 days, CC will make a full disclosure of the invention to those employees and agents of EE who shall be designated by EE as its representatives. CC shall explain the structure and operation of the invention, and shall answer to the best of its ability all questions asked by EE representatives, which may advance their technical understanding of the invention. CC shall submit to EE all writings relating to the invention. Under no circumstances shall EE photocopy the aforementioned writings. CC shall furnish, upon request by EE, any additional information or assistance reasonably necessary to enable EE representatives to understand and evaluate the novelty and utility of the invention.

3.   Confidential Data. EE agrees that all knowledge and information acquired from CC respecting its invention shall be for all time and for all purposes regarded as strictly confidential and EE shall not directly or indirectly disclose said knowledge or information to anyone without the express written consent of CC.

4.   Nonuse Covenant. In the event EE does not desire to purchase, manufacture, distribute, or otherwise utilize said invention, EE agrees that it will not make, use or sell invention or products, processes and/or services derived from examining CC's invention or from CC's disclosure of the concept and idea, whether or not patentable, including, but not limited to, processes, methods, formulas, and techniques, as well as improvements or know-how, whether or not within the scope of the invention.

5.   Representations by EE. EE, in the event that it does not desire to purchase, manufacture, distribute, or otherwise utilize said invention, represents the following:

   a.   It shall return promptly all the original writings submitted by CC to CC's representatives.

   b.   It shall instruct its representatives to hold in strict confidence all information received by CC until such information is available to the public generally or its competitors.

    c.   The proprietary information given to EE's designated representatives, as provided above, shall not be used by EE, embodied in any of its products or exploited in any way by EE. Proprietary information means information, whether written or oral, identified as proprietary and not generally available to the public.

It shall not include the following:

    i.   Information, which at the time of disclosure, had been previously published.

    ii.   Information, which is published after disclosure unless such publication is a breach of this agreement.

    iii.   Information which, prior to disclosure to EE, was already in its possession as evidenced by written records kept in the ordinary course of business by EE or by proof of actual use by EE.

    iv.   Information which, subsequent to disclosure, is obtained by EE from a third person who is lawfully in possession of such information, and not in violation of any contractual, legal, or fiduciary obligation to CC with respect to such information and who does not require EE to refrain from disclosing or using such information.

6.   Breach and Remedies. In the event of a breach of any term or covenant hereof by EE, CC, at any time thereafter, may pursue remedies in both law and equity, including injunctive relief.

7.   Integrated Agreement. This agreement represents the entire understanding and agreement between the parties hereto and supersedes all prior agreements and understandings, either oral or written, between them, with respect to the subject matter hereof. Any modifications of this agreement must be in writing and signed by all the parties hereto.

8.   Governing Law. This agreement, and all transactions contemplated hereby, shall be governed by, construed and enforced in accordance with the laws of the State of HH. The parties herein waive trial by jury and agree to submit to the personal jurisdiction and venue of a court of subject matter jurisdiction located in II County, State of HH. In the event that litigation results from or arises out of this agreement or the performance thereof, the parties agree to reimburse the prevailing party's reasonable attorney's fees, court costs, and all other expenses, whether or not taxable by the court as costs, in addition to any other relief to which the prevailing party may be entitled. In such event, no action shall be entertained by said court or any court of competent jurisdiction if filed more than one year subsequent to the date the cause(s) of action actually accrued, regardless of whether damages were otherwise as of said time calculable.

IN WITNESS WHEREOF, the parties have hereunto set their hands and seal the day and year first above written.

_____

CC Signature	Date

_____

DD Signature	Printed Name	Date

Work-for-hire

Work-for-hire Agreements are a combination of a contract for services along with a nondisclosure agreement all rolled into one. They are normally used when the interface between the inventor and another party goes past the discussion stage and requires some form of actual work be accomplished on a subcontract basis.

They are used to mutually agree that when a subcontractor performs work for you, on what you consider proprietary development, and which may produce derivative works or products that might be of interest to you, that:

1. All of the work, including derivative work or new ideas that are created as a result of working on your idea, are yours, not theirs.

2. That you and you alone have the exclusive rights to them.

Because of recent rulings in the software industry, Work-for-hire Agreements have become an essential part of an inventor's process for assuring the rights to development efforts are not given away.

The courts have recently ruled that without a written Work-for-hire Agreement that your subcontracted work could come under ownership dispute and that you could unknowingly be hiring a partner for all future exploitation of your ideas.

Work-for-hire Agreements spell out, in as much pertinent detail as necessary, the terms of the employment or subcontract agreement and what rights, if any, the employee or subcontractor would have to new works that were derived from the original work that was contracted for.

Description of Work-for-hire Agreement

Pertinent information in Work-for-hire Agreements should include:

AA: The name of employee or independent contractor.

BB: Is the name of the person (inventor) or organization that is hiring the independent contractor.

CC: The date the work is to be completed.

DD: The state in which contract is executed.

Three detailed attachments:

Attachment A: Payment Schedule. In this attachment, you must describe, in exact detail, when AA will be paid and in what manner payment will be made. You must also define what will constitute a mutually agreed upon milestone or task that will signify that a particular payment is due and payable.

Attachment B: Duties. Here you must illustrate what AA has to produce, in order to get paid, by describing the work in detail. Besides the actual work, what AA may be expected to deliver such as detailed specifications, documentation, and so forth? In this attachment, you list what your responsibilities, as the client, will be in addition to payment of AA's invoice. These include providing hardware, technical specifications, workspace, or other mutually agreed upon components that will be required for AA to complete the task as defined

Attachment C: Work Schedule. Here you must describe, in task-by-task detail, the payment of the monies described in Attachment A and the work described in Attachment B, in a time oriented task outline. These tasks should include the delivery of and payment for all of the data, documentation, drawings, tooling, and other support elements that are considered to be a part of the overall project that the client is paying for.

Work-for-hire Agreement

INTRODUCTION: This is a Work-for-hire Agreement in which AA, an independent contractor, agrees to provide services to BB. BB shall pay AA according to the payment schedule set forth in Attachment A of this agreement, which is incorporated by reference herein.

DUTIES: AA agrees to provide the services for BB as per the specifications set forth in Attachment B to this agreement, which is incorporated by reference herein. BB shall supply AA all items listed in Attachment B prior to CC.

OWNERSHIP: In consideration for payment as set forth in Attachment A of this agreement, AA hereby assigns all rights in the work performed under this agreement to BB, including the right to apply for any and all appropriate patents, trademarks, trade secrets and/or copyrights that may result as a consequence of the work performed in BB's name.

AA understands that the work contracted for and described herein is a work-for-hire, which shall be the exclusive property of BB.

Consistent with AA's recognition of BB's complete ownership rights in the work described in Attachment B, AA agrees not to use the work created under this agreement for the benefit of any party other than BB.

COMPLETION DATE: AA agrees to complete all work as per the schedule set forth in Attachment C of this agreement, which is hereby incorporated by reference herein.

TRADE SECRETS: All types of information relating to the work described herein and contracted for, including this agreement and its attachments, are to be considered the trade secrets of BB.

AA shall keep all trade secrets of BB confidential, and shall sign nondisclosure agreements when requested by BB.

ARBITRATION: Any dispute relating to the interpretation or performance of this agreement shall be resolved at the request of either party through binding arbitration. Arbitration shall be conducted in the state of DD in accordance with the then existing rules of the American Arbitration Association. Judgment upon any award by the arbitrators may be entered by the state or federal court having jurisdiction. The parties intend that this agreement to arbitrate be irrevocable.

GENERAL PROVISIONS

- AA may neither subcontract nor hire persons to aid in the contracted work without the prior written consent of BB.

- Any modifications to this agreement must be in writing and signed by both parties.

AA Signature   Date

BB Signature   Date

Attachment A: Payment Schedule

AA shall be paid in the following manner:

Attachment B: Duties

AA will be responsible for:

BB will be responsible for:

Attachment C: Work Schedule

AA agrees to complete the work described in Attachment B according to the following schedule:

Non-Competition

When dealing with proprietary information that was acquired at significant cost to you and/or your organization, it might be desirable to restrict employees who leave your employ from using the information by going to work for a competitor.

This agreement called a non-competition agreement and as an employer, you are entitled to require those who perform work for you, as an employee, to sign one as a condition of their employment.

Although the agreement looks like it totally favors the employer, it must be used carefully or it will not be honored as the courts frown on taking away a person's means of making a living.

The restrictions that you impose, which are those, which you can enforce, must not restrict the employee's ability to make a living. They are enforceable only on something that was developed at your expense and is considered to be proprietary knowledge.

For example, if a sales employee develops a customer list based on the sales of a specific product that is proprietary to your organization, and the list is to be used for aftermarket sales, the knowledge of the list, and its subsequent usage, is restricted to the organization that paid for its development because the employer paid for it through their direct marketing efforts. This situation can be covered and enforced under a non-competition agreement.

On the other hand, if you use the yellow pages of the phone book to develop a list of potential clients, there is no proprietary aspect to the list (since it is publicly available) and there can be no restrictions imposed or enforced or used on this list.

The same logic applies to restricting an employee's ability to work for a competitor. The only thing that the employee can be restricted from doing is using specific knowledge obtained while in your employ, that was considered to be proprietary to you, as the employer.

Non-Competition Agreement

FOR GOOD CONSIDERATION, said consideration being or having been rendered by the COMPANY, I, the undersigned, hereby agree that upon my conclusion of business with the COMPANY that I shall not compete with the business of the COMPANY, or its successors or assigns.

The term not compete as used in this agreement means that I shall not directly or indirectly, as an owner, officer, director, employee, consultant, or stockholder, engage in a business substantially similar or competitive to the business of the company.

This non-compete agreement shall extend only for a radius of _____ miles from the present location of the COMPANY, and shall be in full force and effect for _____ years, commencing with the date of conclusion of my services.

_____

Signature   Date

Company

_____

Name

_____

Address

_____

City   State   ZIP

Contingent Commitment

One of the areas of concern to inventors is when they find themselves in a situation where they have an original idea that has not yet been developed and under the current laws, have no formal protection, but still need to disclose their ideas to another party or organization for purposes of mutual benefit.

The solution to this dilemma comes in the form of a seldom publicized, but widely used document known as a Contingent Commitment Agreement whose name pretty much sums up what it's all about:

1. It's an agreement.

2. It involves commitments on the part of both parties.

3. There are contingencies involved on the part of both parties.

Contingent Commitment Agreements are used to establish a mutually agreed upon value and a potential payment for knowledge and information that will result in a certain level or standard of performance, prior to divulging the specific information regarding the precise method for obtaining the desired result.

To give you an example of how they came about, consider a business plan for a new start-up enterprise. Until the business is started, there are no funds to hire critical employees. Without the critical employees to make the company viable, venture capitalists will not fund the new start-up. This is the perfect example of the old adage: Which came first—the chicken or the egg?

Here's how the problem has been handled and where the basic tenants of the agreement came from. The individual or group creating the business plan for the new start-up would advertise and interview for the needed key employees. Once the individual was found, both parties would sign an agreement that stated the following:

- The person writing the plan would be allowed to insert the resume' and qualifications of the selected individual into the plan.

- If the plan was funded, the person writing the plan committed to hire the individual whose resume' was added to the plan.

- The person whose resume' was included with the plan committed to quitting their current job and joining the new start-up organization as soon as the funding was in place.

Inventors have a similar problem when they reach a point where in order to obtain support, financing, or some other form of mutual profitability, the inventor must disclose to the other party, certain pertinent details of the idea or concept which once divulged, could be exploited without the involvement of the inventor.

Since the concept is incomplete, the inventor is not in a position, for whatever the reason, to obtain proprietary protection under the current intellectual property laws.

For inventors, the basic tenants of the agreement reflect the following:

- The inventor has an idea or concept that he or she believes is of value to the other party.

- The inventor needs to disclose the information to the other party to obtain support.

- The inventor wants the other party to provide support if what they say is accurate and of interest to the other party.

- If the representations of the inventor are true, the other party agrees to become involved in whatever manner is agreed upon. If the representations are not true, are already known to the other party, or are not of interest to the other party, the other party is prohibited from exploiting the idea or innovation without the inventor.

In other words, the inventor agrees to tell the other party what the idea will accomplish but not the specifics of how it is accomplished until both parties sign the agreement.

As with the other contractual documents outlined above, the Contingent Commitment Agreement is a legal contractual document that can be used in a court of law to recover damages if the need arises.

Description of Contingent Commitment Agreement

The Contingent Commitment Agreement contains the following items:

AA: Date of the agreement (day, month and year i.e. 21st of May, 2005).

BB: Person or organization that is offering to divulge the information.

CC: Person or organization that is agreeing to receive the information.

DD: A full description of the relative merits and/or benefits of the idea or innovation including any sub-points.

EE: A description of the mutually agreed upon compensation including any sub-points.

FF: A signature of an independent, disinterested, third party who will attest, by signing the document, to the veracity of the statements contained in the document including the willingness of the parties involved to sign the document without coercion.

Contingent Commitment Agreement

AA

This is an agreement between BB and CC, which outlines the basic guidelines for a Contingent Commitment Agreement. The purpose of this agreement is to allow BB to disclose an idea and/or product to CC for the purpose of review, discussion, and the possibility of a mutually beneficial business relationship.

The basic tenants of this agreement are as follows:

1.   BB represents to CC the following: DD

2.   CC agrees to the following:

   a.   That if the representations presented by BB are, in fact, truthful and are of interest to CC, that CC aggress to enter into an agreement with terms and conditions to be negotiated to the mutual satisfaction of both parties.

   b.   That in the event that mutually satisfactory licensing arrangements are not reached by BB and CC, that CC:

   •   Shall have no rights or obligations under this agreement.

- Agrees that all designs, ideas, and intellectual property disclosed during this relationship are, and shall remain, the proprietary and exclusive property of BB.

- Will not use, cause to be used, or disclose, in any manner whatsoever, these proprietary items, and

- That all physical items including, but not limited to, prototypes, drawings, descriptions, and/or any manner of documentation or design which could be used to transfer the design characteristics represented in this agreement, shall not be kept, copied or distributed but shall, instead, be presented to BB at no charge to BB for his sole and exclusive use.

c. If the information, products, or materials presented and discussed by BB and CC during this meeting, or if the information, products, or materials presented and discussed by BB and CC during this meeting were known to CC prior to the disclosure referenced herein by BB, that CC shall be under no obligation to compensate BB and that CC's sole obligation shall be that of confidentiality of the information, products, or materials presented and discussed by BB and CC during this meeting or meetings with the exception of the following conditions:

- Information, which at the time of disclosure, had been previously published or a matter of public record.

- Information that is published after disclosure unless such publication is a breach of this agreement.

- Information, which, prior to disclosure to CC was already in its possession, as evidenced by written records kept in the ordinary course of business by or by proof of actual use by CC.

- Information which, subsequent to disclosure, is obtained by CC from a third person who is lawfully in possession of such information, and not in violation of any contractual, legal, or fiduciary obligation to BB with respect to such information and who does not require CC to refrain from disclosing or using such information.

In the event that CC violates any term or covenant contained herein, BB, at any time thereafter, may pursue legal action in both law and equity, including injunctive relief.

This agreement represents the entire understanding and agreement between the parties hereto and supersedes all prior agreements and understandings, either oral or written, between them, with respect to the subject matter hereof. Any modification s of this agreement must be in writing and signed by all the parties hereto.

BB Signature   Date

CC Signature   Date

FF Signature   Printed Name   Date

Licensing

The licensing agreement is the document that is used to completely outline everything, in detail, as to what the licensee will do and what the inventor will receive.

Make no mistake about these agreements; they are long, involved, complicated, and necessary to ensure that neither part is exploited and that all of the contingencies of the relationship are completely defined and agreed to.

Experience has shown that these agreements are the primary reason why inventors are exploited without proper compensation. In short, they are the legal minefields of the invention industry.

Inventors are overly concerned with the disclosure of their invention and having it exploited by the parties they disclosed to. Although this has happened in the past, and will occur again in the future, it actually happens so seldom that it is of minor concern, or should be, to the inventor.

Conversely, the greatest occurrence of inequitable exploitation of inventors and their inventions seems to occur during the licensing phase wherein the licensee employs a variety of tactics to negotiate the value to the inventor right out of the deal.

I spent many years in the toy business where I saw good deals, bad deals, and deals that could have been good, go bad because the licensing agreement was not fully understood, properly drafted or executed.

You must have the guidance of someone who is experienced in the licensing process. It's not what's in a contract that causes problems, but what's left out and open to interpretation!

This guidance is not necessarily an attorney unless the individual or firm has specific experience in licensing agreements. If they do not have the experience or leave something undefined or uncovered, you, as the inventor, will eventually pay the price for their ignorance.

Bear in mind that this is ONLY A SAMPLE and should NOT be used without the modification and supervision of someone who knows and understands how to prepare and negotiate a licensing agreement.

Description of Licensing Agreement

The Licensing Agreement is used when an individual (or a company) wants to grant the rights to manufacture, market, distribute, and/or utilize something which an individual (or a company) owns or controls the rights.

For example, if an individual owns the rights to a new product, by virtue of the fact that the inventor invented it, and wanted to license a company the exclusive rights to manufacture and market the invention, then a Licensing Agreement would be used. There are several contractual clauses in the agreement. These may be modified or changed as the parties involved see fit.

All clauses, details, terms, conditions, etc. should be read and reviewed by competent counsel prior to the finalization and signing of any agreement. In addition to any custom modifications that the parties may wish to make, there are 28 basic blanks that need to be filled in on this agreement:

AA: Is the name of the manufacturer, which is desirous of obtaining the rights.

BB: Is the state in which AA declares to be their primary location for doing business.

CC: Is the legal address of AA.

DD: Is the shortened name of AA.

EE: Is the name of the person (inventor) or organization that is licensing the company the rights to use, manufacture, market, etc. the property to which he controls the rights.

FF: Is the legal address of EE.

GG: Is the shortened name of EE.

HH: Is the date of execution of the licensing agreement (day, month, year).

II: Is the given name, title, registered name, etc. that is being used, at the time of the execution of the licensing agreement.

JJ: Is a definitive description of the property being licensed.

KK: Is a definitive description of all the currently known ways, techniques, materials, etc. that may be utilized to create the property being licensed.

LL: Is a mutually agreed amount of money that is to be paid to GG by DD as a non-refundable advance against future royalties that are assumed to be forthcoming.

MM: Specifies the number of days, within which, the advance monies are to be paid by DD to GG.

NN: Is the negotiated percentage of billings that are due and payable to GG by DD in return for the rights licensed by GG to DD.

OO: Is a negotiated amount of money that GG is to submit to DD in order to repurchase the rights as granted under the licensing agreement to DD in the event that DD fails to actively pursue the tenants of the licensing agreement.

PP: Specifies a quantity of the property which, if said quantity of sales falls below, constitutes an inactive property, and which gives cause for GG to exercise the repurchase rights as defined in the licensing agreement.

QQ: A specified amount of time required.

RR: A specified labor rate to be charged.

SS: A mutually agreed upon number of calendar days.

UU: A mutually agreed upon number of calendar days.

VV: A mutually agreed upon number of calendar days.

WW: A mutually agreed upon number of calendar days.

XX: A mutually agreed upon number of calendar days.

YY: A mutually agreed upon dollar value.

ZZ: A mutually agreed upon percentage.

ZZ: A mutually agreed upon percentage.

aa: State in which the agreement is signed.

bb: A mutually agreed upon dollar value.

Licensing Agreement

I.   This is a licensing agreement between AA, a company doing business under the laws of the State of BB and located at CC referred to as DD and EE, an individual doing business at FF hereafter referred to as GG, made and entered into this HH of HH, HH.

This is a Licensing Agreement for the following item, including any other forms, modifications, portions and accessories thereof, hereafter referred to as the item.

The item is to be provided by GG and is defined as follows: II

JJ
KK

II.   Rights Granted

1.   GG hereby warrants that he/she is the assignee and current, exclusive owner of the item and all derivative works and therefore has the exclusive rights to this item and herein grants to DD the exclusive license to manufacture, distribute, sell and otherwise deal in the item during the term of this agreement, and in addition grants DD these rights under all patents, trademarks, trade secrets and copyrights now or hereafter owned or assigned to GG relating to the item.

2.   The item may be manufactured in numerous configurations including, but not limited to, material, size and design changes that serve to enhance the appearance, performance, and overall salability of the item.

3.   Prior to any modifications and/or changes from the original design(s) of the item by DD, DD shall submit said modifications, changes, and/or revised specifications to GG for approval.

4.   Upon receipt of proposed changes, revisions, and/or modifications, GG shall review said changes and notify DD, in writing, of his/her approval or disapproval, with appropriate notes and explanations and recommended modifications if disapproved, within ten calendar days of the receipt of said changes, revisions, and/or modifications.

5.   Unless and until GG approves such changes, revisions, and/or modifications of the item in writing, DD is prohibited from advertising, manufacturing, offering, selling, or otherwise engaging in the representation of the revised item.

6. This grant is effective throughout the United States of America and all foreign countries as currently deemed acceptable trading partners, or that shall be deemed acceptable trading partners during the active life of this agreement, by the United States Department of Commerce.

7. The rights and license herein granted shall include all inventions, improvements, enhancements and modifications to the item made or conceived during the term of this agreement and all, patents, trademarks, trade secrets and/or copyrights applications based on or covering the same, which GG owns or controls or hereafter may own or control, including, without limitation, presently anticipated improvements to the item.

8. GG hereby guarantees the validity of the claims proffered in the agreement for the overall accuracy of the item if, and only if, DD makes no changes, additions, deletions, corrections or alterations to the item as delivered. In the event that the item is modified without the express written permission of GG, GG assumes no responsibility for failures or alterations of performance of the item due to noncompliance with said guidelines.

III. Support

1. GG will provide DD with copies of documents indicating his/her rights and copies of patents, trademarks, trade secrets and copyrights if applicable.

2. GG will furnish to DD all information and documents regarding the item and any improvements including, without limitation, complete details of manufacturing and reproduction procedures, including detailed specifications of processes and products; complete specifications, including supplier/vendor identification of materials and components used in manufacture; detailed designs used in manufacture; drawings, specifications, data and other materials currently under his possession and/or control that may be required to assist or facilitate in the effective production development, manufacture, and marketing of the item.

3. GG agrees to supply DD with his/her services, at no charge, in the development, of the item. Said services shall not exceed QQ hours of time. In the event that additional time is required for matters pertaining to the promotion of the item, DD shall compensate GG at a rate of $RR per actual hour spent working on the item, with a minimum billing of eight hours of time for each occurrence of the services, whether on-site at DD, by phone, e-mail, or in person-to-person meetings as agreed by mutual arrangement, or at a location that is deemed as mutually acceptable for GG to perform said services.

4. This fee shall be renegotiated annually and said services shall be offered by GG to DD, under the terms and conditions of this agreement, for as long as the item remains active as defined by this agreement. In addition to these charges, DD agrees to compensate GG for all mutually agreed upon out-of-pocket expenses.

IV. Royalties and Expenses

1. In return for the licensing of the exclusive rights to the item, DD agrees to compensate GG royalties as follows:

    A. Upon the execution of this agreement, DD shall pay to GG a nonrefundable good faith advance in the amount of $LL toward future royalty payments, within MM days, as defined in this agreement.

    B. DD shall offset this $LL against the first of payments otherwise due GG under this agreement.

    C. Additional royalties equal to NN percent of "net receipts" of the "sales" of the item shall be paid to GG during the active life of the item. "Sales" shall mean the gross money received by DD for the sale of the item exclusive of sales, use, excise, and other taxes, packing, insurance, shipping, and other similar charges reimbursed by customers from all sales of the item less:

        a. The amount of any credits or refunds for returns, taking into account any reserves for bad debts or returns previously established by DD and

        b. Any provisions for credit, discounts, rebates, and promotional allowances to customers and

        c. The amount of any sales or use taxes required to be paid or withheld by DD with respect to the payment due GG.

2. "Sales" shall mean the actual accumulated sales of items, including, but not limited to all cash collections, bank transfers of funds and receipts of valuable consideration. Unpaid invoices, promotional allowances, etc. shall not be considered as a "sale".

3. Royalties will be paid quarterly. Royalties will be paid within 30 days after the end of each calendar quarter for all items shipped during that quarter. Royalty payments shall be accompanied by a statement setting forth the number of items sold, the gross sales, the net sales and the royalties due for the stated period, as reflected by DD's books of accounts.

4. GG shall be entitled to reimbursement from DD for software, hardware, travel, and other expenses, in the amounts incurred, in support of the development and marketing of the item but only if such expenses are pre-approved in writing by DD. GG shall present to DD written documentation of such pre-approved expenses and the amounts incurred and DD shall reimburse GG for such pre-approved expenses within 30 calendar days.

V.   Activity

1. This agreement shall be considered active and commence on the date of mutual signing of this agreement and shall continue for as long as the item shall continue to be manufactured and sold, unless sooner terminated under provisions of this agreement.

2. This licensing agreement shall continue for as long as the item is active. The item shall be considered as being active under the following terms and provisions:

    A. Testing: DD shall complete the development, testing and evaluation of pre-production versions of the item and all related packaging, advertising, promotional, and collateral materials within SS calendar days of the written approval of this agreement.

    B. Tooling: DD shall commence production tooling of the item within TT calendar days of the written approval of this agreement. Said production tooling shall be completed no later than UU calendar days from the written approval of this document.

    C. Advertising: DD shall begin actively advertising and promoting the item within VV days of the written approval of this document.

    D. Manufacturing: DD shall begin the active manufacture of production ready items within WW days of the written approval of this document.

    E. Sales: Once active sale of the item commences, it shall be considered as an active product so long as the gross revenues for the sale of the item exceed $XX per calendar quarter.

    F. DD will have the exclusive rights to determine both the wholesale and suggested retail-selling price of the item.

VI. Reversion Rights

1. GG may, under any one of the following circumstances, and only under the following circumstances, repurchase all rights to the item from DD for the sum of $OO paid to DD:

    A. Failure by DD to actively develop the tooling, testing, advertising and manufacturing materials for the item as defined above.

    B. Failure by DD to actively offer the item for sale, as defined above.

    C. Upon notification or announcement by DD that the item is being dropped DD's line of products.

    D. Total sales of the item in any four consecutive quarters, following initial release of the item, totals less than PP.

2. This agreement is automatically terminated if DD ceases to do business and all rights and assignments, as defined herein, shall automatically revert to, and become, the sole and exclusive rights of GG.

3. If improvements to the item, whether original or derived, or deemed as functionally advantageous changes are made to the item, subsequent to the execution of this agreement, by joint efforts of GG and DD, said improvements shall become the property of GG and shall become a part of the active elements of this agreement including any and all royalty and reversion clauses including the right of GG to purchase the rights to the item, including any and all improvements made to the item, for the sum of $1.00 under the terms and conditions of this agreement.

4. Any and all such ideas, modifications, and/or improvements made to the item by GG during the active life of this agreement as defined herein, shall be offered to DD, in a timely fashion, so as to provide DD with the right of first refusal to incorporate, purchase, license, and use said ideas, modifications, and/or improvements in the development, manufacture and/or sale of the item. Said improvements shall not be considered as automatically falling under the terms and conditions of this agreement but shall be negotiated as a separate item of business consequence.

5. In accepting the right of first refusal under the terms and conditions of this agreement, DD agrees to review and either accept or decline said products within 14 days of submission by GG to DD. In the event that DD does not respond to said offer within the 14 days as agreed to, the right to said products(s) offered shall be assumed to belong exclusively to GG and DD shall not have or assume to have any rights to the product(s) submitted.

VII. Audit Rights

1. DD agrees to keep full and accurate books of accounts and records reflecting the manufacture and sale of the item. GG shall have the right to inspect DD's records a maximum of twice a year giving DD reasonable notice to verify the accuracy of the royalty payments that may be due hereunder.

2. This right of inspection shall include the right to make pertinent copies or extracts. All information in DD's records shall be considered confidential.

VIII. Confidentiality, Proprietary Rights and Recourse

1. Each party shall treat as confidential and proprietary the confidential and proprietary information of the other party to this agreement, and each party shall maintain the confidentiality of it.

2. Notwithstanding any provision of this agreement to the contrary, the item shall also be defined to include any and all related trade secrets and confidential information associated with the item and any improvements or enhancements thereon, and accordingly, all such related trade secrets and confidential information shall also be included within the scope of this agreement.

3. In the event DD elects to prepare and submit patents, trademarks, trade secrets or copyrights applications for any improvements on the item, GG agrees and understands that if so requested GG will cooperate with such attorneys as DD may designate to accomplish the successful filing of said patents, trademarks, trade secrets and copyrights.

4. GG shall render to DD such services in a consulting capacity at a rate of $bb per actual hour spent working on the item, with a minimum billing of eight hours of time for each occurrence of the services, whether on-site at DD, by phone, e-mail, or in person-to-person meetings as agreed by mutual arrangement, or at a location that is deemed as mutually acceptable for GG to perform said services, for the preparation and submission of trademarks or copyright applications.

5. This fee shall be renegotiated annually and said services shall be offered by GG to DD, under the terms and conditions of this agreement, for as long as the item remains active as defined by this agreement. In addition to these charges, DD agrees to compensate GG for all mutually agreed upon out-of-pocket expenses.

6. During the term of this agreement, GG grants DD the right to bring and pursue infringement actions against third parties that DD believes to be infringing upon the rights created by the item's patents, trademarks, trade

secrets and/or copyrights at DD's sole expense.

7.   At his/her discretion, GG may join in any infringement action and cooperate with DD in the pursuit thereof notwithstanding any provision of this agreement to the contrary.

IX.   Assignment, Sublicense, and Sale

1.   This agreement is not assignable or sub-licensable by DD unless such assignment is reviewed and approved, in writing, prior to said assignment by GG, and providing that the assignment is not in default of any provisions.

2.   GG and DD agree that no rights to the item may be sold or transferred except by mutual agreement and upon terms and conditions mutually acceptable to GG and DD.

3.   If, by mutual agreement between GG and DD, the complete rights to the item are sold, then GG shall receive YY percent of the sale and/or royalty proceeds and DD shall receive ZZ percent the sale and/or royalty proceeds.

X.   Indemnification

1.   This agreement does not create a partnership or joint venture between the parties and DD shall not have power to obligate or bind GG in any manner whatsoever nor shall GG have the right to bind DD in any manner.

2.   DD shall hold GG harmless from and against and indemnify GG of all liability, loss, costs, expenses or damages caused by any reason of any items (whether or not defective) or any act or commission of DD, including but not limited to any injury (whether to body, property, personal, business character or reputation) sustained by any person or to any person or to property, and for infringement of any patents, trademarks, trade secrets or copyrights or other rights of third parties, and for any violation of municipal, state or federal laws or regulations governing the products or their sale, which may result from the sale, distribution, and/or operation of the item by DD under the terms stated in this agreement.

XI.   Termination

1.   DD may terminate this agreement at any time by furnishing GG with written notice of its intentions and reasons for termination. Such termination shall not effect DD's obligation to pay any and all royalties owed to GG.

2.   In the event that an act of government, war conditions, fire, flood or labor problems prevent either party from performing in accordance with the provisions of this agreement, such nonperformance shall be excused and shall not be considered a breach so long as that condition prevails.

3.   In the event of termination, unless termination is due to default by DD in its obligation to render timely royalty payments and statements, DD may dispose of items which are on hand or in the process at the time of termination for a period of 180 days after termination, provided that payments and statements are rendered when due.

4.   Upon termination of this agreement, all rights, title and interest in the item, transferred herein by GG shall revert to GG at no cost to GG. DD shall not thereafter manufacture, sell, or otherwise deal in the item.

XII.   Provisos, Notification, and Governing Law

1.   If any provisions of this agreement are found for any reason to be invalid, the validity of the remaining provisions shall not be affected thereby.

2.   All notices required pursuant to this agreement shall be in writing and shall be sent certified mail to the addresses set forth above or any other address either party may designate and shall be deemed given when received.

3. Any provision of this agreement which in any way contravenes applicable law, shall to the extent of such contravention, be deemed severed and of no effect, but the other provisions of this agreement shall continue in full force and effect, to the fullest extent allowed by applicable law.

4. This agreement shall be governed, construed and enforced in accordance with the laws of the State of aa in all respects.

5. Any notices or other communications required or committed hereunder shall be deemed given when personally delivered or upon receipt, after having been sent by personal hand delivery or overnight courier such as, but not limited to, Federal Express, and if to licensor addressed as follows:

   GG Address.

   If to licensee addressed to it as follows:

   DD Address

6. This agreement comprises the entire understanding between GG and DD and no change, modification or wavers of any of the provisions hereof shall be valid unless in writing and signed by the parties.

7. This agreement shall be binding upon and shall inure to the benefit of the parties hereto and their successors, heirs or assigns.

XIII. Execution

IN WITNESS WHEREOF, the parties have executed this agreement as of the day and year first above written.

LICENSOR:

_____

GG Signature   Date

LICENSEE

_____

DD Signature   Date

Chapter 5
Patents

One of the first concerns of inventors is how to get their idea patented. Although the process is real and has been granted to over six million ideas so far, it's just one of the three federal registration processes that grants proprietary rights to an inventor: patents, trademarks and copyrights.

Furthermore, there is a list of reasons, both logical and practical, why you might not want to get a federal registration on your invention.

That having been stated, lets get started.

First patent granted was in 1790 for potash

Of all the topics I address, this is the most misunderstood, misrepresented, and over exploited of all of the tools available to inventors for establishing their proprietary rights to an invention.

If that statement sounds harsh, it's meant to be. Not because I'm opposed to patents, which I am not, but because the tool has been so misrepresented and misused that I automatically question is applicability to any inventor's goal of exploiting his or her invention for profit.

Because of my dual existences as an engineer and a marketer, I've been forced to do my homework on the entire intellectual property arena because my livelihood in both vocations has depended on it.

Although I have a vested interest in your success as an inventor, I do NOT have any vesting in which of the processes or tools that you use to achieve success. If I had such an interest, I might slant my opinions in that direction. Since I don't, you'll get the most objective viewpoint available from a profitability standpoint.

Let's start with some realities and current statistics, which came from the April 2002 issue of Wired magazine:

1. Patentability has nothing to do with marketability or profitability. The three elements are mutually exclusive.

    • Patentability is the right to establish the proprietary ownership to an idea.

    • Marketability is when you can convince other people to buy the idea.

    • Profitability is when you actually make an income from your idea.

2. Of the six million patents issued in the history of the USPTO, less than 1 percent has been marketed.

3. Of the more than one million patents in force today, less than 5 percent of them are or ever will be licensed or earn royalties.

4. Some 500,000 of these patents will expire halfway though their 20-year life spans because the inventors or companies that registered them will have stopped paying the maintenance fees.

5. Of all the products available in the marketplace today, far less than 1 percent have a patent.

The Gazette is a weekly USPTO publication that lists all patents that issued during that week. The Gazette also lists all patents that expired during the week due to nonpayment of maintenance fees. Based on periodic checks of this section, it appears that well over one-third of independent inventors are letting their patents expire with the first maintenance fee payable.

Sound scary? Weird? Unbelievable? Well believe them because they're true. If they're true, why the great rush to patent before going to market? And where did the concept of patentability being linked with marketability and profitability come from? Are they blatant lies?

The final answer is both yes and no, depending on whom you talk to, when you talk to them, and what they're talking about (assuming they know what they're talking about!).

The first inequity is that the word patent has become a cliché for several different things. Probably the closest definition that you'll want to consider for obtaining a patent is: open to public inspection while under the control of a particular individual or party.

This definition means that you, as the patent holder, are in control of the invention, under whatever laws pertain to the item, even though it is available to the public.

This is pretty good although in reality, there is probably nothing available that exactly fits the definition of what inventors would like a patent to be. So I'm going to explain the realities of the process to you and you can decide for yourself what's what and if a patent is the appropriate tool for you to use.

What do bulletproof vests, fire escapes, windshield wipers, and laser printers all have in common?
Women invented them all.

What is a patent?

A patent is a grant of rights to the innovator or creator of a new idea, product or process. Patents are granted by the USPTO in Washington, DC.

To be granted a patent, your idea must be deemed as novel and useful by a patent examiner. Novel is defined as never having been done that way before. Useful means that the innovation serves some form of useful purpose. In the case of design patents, decorative is accepted as useful.

What qualifies for a patent?

I've heard all the same stories that you have like: It must have seven significant changes or at least 20 percent difference in order to qualify for a new patent.

None of these are true because the granting of a patent is very subjective. If the patent examiners believe that your idea is novel and useful, they will award you the patent. Period!

The patent examiner who grants patents receive training on evaluating new ideas for their true novelty but when all is said and done, it's a judgment call on the part of a human being, which determines whether your idea is granted a patent.

A patent examiner will review the patent application that you submit for your idea and the examiner's judgment will be the sole determining factor as to whether or not you are granted the patent.

It has little or nothing to do with how much or how many changes have been made but rather whether the examiner believes that your idea is novel enough to be considered as qualifying for a new patent.

What are patents granted for?

Patents are generally granted for the way something is accomplished rather than what it accomplishes.

Let's look at an example using a wrench. A wrench is a basic tool that's used to tighten and loosen nuts and bolts. Realistically, all wrenches do the same thing, tighten and loosen bolts, but wrench A uses a different design and/or mechanism to accomplish the effort from wrench B, and wrench C has a different mechanism or design from wrenches A and B.

For purposes of patenting, it's the difference between the wrenches that carries the concept of novelty and usefulness and it is that specific difference that is patented—not the application or use of the tool itself.

Here's a note—if we were able to specify the use for the wrench, it would be called an application patent and there is no such patent. What you use the device for is irrelevant to the patent process.

Once again, what is patented is the specific concept that is used to achieve a desired result.

Patent Length and Maintenance Fees

Patents do not last forever. The laws regarding the life of a patent are constantly being changed and are currently set at 14 years for a design patent and 20 years for a plant patent or a utility patent.

Once granted, a maintenance fees may have to be paid to the USPTO to keep the patent active.

For maintenance fees, the rules are as follows:

- Maintenance fees apply only to utility patents—not to design or plant patents.

- They apply to all utility patents based on applications filed on or after December 12, 1980. The small entity rules (as of February 1, 2007) (half-rate fees for small entities) apply—the fees listed below are for **small entities**:

  - The first maintenance fee of $450 is due (received by the USPTO) by 3½ years following the issue date. If not received, the patent will expire at 4 years.

  - The second maintenance fee of $1,150 is due by 7½ years following the issue date. If not received, the patent will expire at 8 years.

- The third maintenance fee of $1,900 is due by 11½ years following the issue date. If not received, the patent will expire at 12 years.

- These fees are not invoiced. It is the responsibility of the inventor to get them in on time. If you miss your due date, you can still pay during the six months prior to patent expiration by adding a $65 surcharge.

- Even after expiration, you may be able to resurrect it—if you can prove to the USPTO that the nonpayment was unavoidable (with an additional $640 surcharge) or unintentional (with an additional $1,500 surcharge).

The USPTO accepts maintenance fee payments by deposit account over the Internet. The USPTO provides customers the capability to pay maintenance fees by credit card or electronic funds transfer (EFT) using the USPTO Internet web site http://www.USPTO.gov.

Your patent attorney usually will calendar the payment of the fee and will notify you appropriately. If you have any questions about this aspect of the patent, discuss this with your patent attorney.

Kinds of Patents

The USPTO issues three types of patent offering different lengths of protection and covering different types of subject. They are plant patents, utility patent and design patent.

Plant Patent

Issued for a new and distinct, invented or discovered asexually reproduced plants including cultivated sprouts, mutants, hybrids, and newly found seedlings, other than a tuber propagated plant or a plant found in an uncultivated state are plant patents.

A quick overview of plant patents tells us that they:

- Are granted on asexually reproduced, distinct, and/or new varieties of plants.

- Take two to five years to be processed.

- Have an active lifetime of 20 years.

- Have no maintenance fees.

- Cost approximately $880 or more per patent for filing fees. The current fees are listed at http://www.USPTO.gov.

Popcorn is a great example of a plant patent. Popcorn is a type of corn that dries out on the outside but has some moisture left on the inside.

When you heat it in hot air or oil, the moisture inside turns to steam and starts to expand. When the pressure gets high enough, the kernel literally explodes and blows itself inside out revealing the tender inner sections that are now cooked and edible.

The only problem with popcorn is that when the kernels have popped, they're now dry and subject to burning if you don't remove them from the heat fairly quickly. This means that from the start to the finish of the batch of popcorn, we need to have all of the popcorn (or as much as possible) complete it's exploding at about the same time.

Logic dictates that if the kernels all contain the same amount of moisture that they'll reach the exploding point at the same time. Unfortunately, this doesn't occur naturally in most popcorn. In fact, if you wait for most of the kernels in a regular batch to pop, the first kernels popped will probably be burned.

Several companies have developed unique strains of popcorn where the kernels all have uniform moisture content. When you pop a batch of this popcorn, the explosions all take place at about the same time and there are very few un-popped kernels when you remove it from the heat.

The unique strain of popcorn is defined by the USPTO as novel (never having been done that way before) and useful (we get to eat it all) so it qualified for a patent.

Utility Patent (MECHANICAL)

Issued for the invention of a new and useful process, machine, manufacture, or composition of matter, or a new and useful improvement are utility patents. This category also covers business method patents.

A quick overview of utility patents tells us that they:

- Are granted on the way something works or a process for achieving a desired result.

- Take two to four years to be processed.

- Have an active lifetime of 20 years.

- Have three maintenance fees.

- Cost approximately $4,800 or more per patent for filing. The current fees are listed at http://www.USPTO.gov.

Since utility patents cover two different things, two examples are in order. The first has to do with the way something works.

You've probably seen one or more of the late night infomercials for tools. One of the niftiest tool ideas is the wrench that automatically adjusts for either US or metric size nuts and bolts by using hexagonally shaped sliding rods to the right dimensions. It's one of the few true examples of one-size fits all.

Notice that this wrench does NOT DO anything different (it tightens and loosens nuts and bolts), but how it gets the job done is novel (new and different) and that's what is claimed in the patent.

Let's look at a process for achieving a desired result. The best and simplest example is a recipe for some popular form of prepackaged food. To get the flavor, consistency, texture, and overall appeal to the consumer, standard ingredients like flour, water, butter, sugar, etc. are mixed together, cooked, and packed for mass consumption.

The manufacturer develops a unique step-by-step process that gives the end product a unique characteristic that makes it popular with consumer, so he decides that this is a good idea and files for a patent to make sure that the competition doesn't copy the method.

If the step-by-step process for achieving the desired result is what makes the product unique, then it's a candidate for a utility patent because if you vary the process, you'll get a different result. Get the idea?

Business method patents are part of a larger family of patents known as utility patents that protect inventions, chemical formulas and other discoveries. A business method is classified as a process because it is not a physical object like a mechanical invention or chemical composition.

Traditionally, the USPTO rarely granted business method patents, claiming that a process could not be patented if it was an abstract idea; something the USPTO believed described most business methods.

These rules changed in July 1998, when a federal court upheld a patent for a method of calculating the net asset value of mutual funds. The court ruled that patent laws were intended to protect any method, whether or not it required the aid of a computer, so long as it produced a "useful, concrete and tangible result."

Thus with one stroke, the court legitimized both software patents and methods of doing business, opening the way for Internet related patents and the USPTO created a new classification for applications: Data processing: financial, business practice, management or cost/price determination.

Design Patent

Issued for a new, original, and ornamental design for an article of manufacture are design patents.

A quick overview of design patents tells us that they:

- Are granted on the way something looks, but on its exterior surfaces only.

- Take one to two years to be processed.

- Have an active lifetime of 14 years.

- Have no maintenance fees.

- Cost approximately $615 or more per patent for filing fees. The current fees are listed at http://www.USPTO.gov.

A great example of a very popular design patent is Apple Computer's Imac design. This is a self-contained computer with a radical design for self-containment of the computer, monitor, and all the accessories. The free flowing lines, curved surfaces, and jellybean color combinations give it a unique look and differentiate it from every other computer system manufactured.

A couple of years after the Imac computers were released, a very popular computer manufacturer released a Windows based PC that looked like the Imac. They figured if the look were so appealing that they'd build a computer that looked like the Imac but didn't have the Macintosh operating system.

Within one month, Apple computer had prevailed on the US Court system and was able to have the entire inventory removed from the marketplace because it violated the proprietary, patented, look of the Imac.

Novelty Search

Whether you decide that a patent is necessary for your needs or not, if you think there is a possibility of your idea being patentable, it's a good idea to have a novelty search performed to make sure that you're not violating somebody else's patent. The novelty search establishes:

1. If there are any existing patents on what you claim.

2. If there is a patent, but it was never maintained or has expired. It now has become public domain and you are free to use it.

3. A potential for patent.

The novelty search is also important so that you don't suddenly end up with a new partner or a potential lawsuit on your hands for infringing on an existing patent.

Special rates can be found for a novelty search for $300 to $600. Rarely do novelty searches run over $1,500.

Patent Agent and Patent Searchers

There are a large number of patent searchers and patent agents who will pull the related patents to your invention. A licensed patent searcher or patent agent is prohibited, by their license, from rendering opinions. Their job is to research and forward the appropriate patents.

This is not to say that a searcher or agent doesn't have excellent judgment in these matters and that their opinions are not as valid as a patent attorney's, but they cannot render an opinion. My recommendation to ensure that you get the most useful information is to ALWAYS use a patent attorney.

Patent Library

The government has several patent libraries throughout the country. There is at least one patent library in each state, frequently more. Call the USPTO for the patent library closest to you.

The public libraries provide access to patent and trademark collections. These collections vary from library to library. All libraries offer various CD-ROM products, which provide access to patent and trademark information.

The librarian will be happy to show you how to research patents and, although it's time consuming, it's actually quite simple once you are familiar with the system of classification and filing.

The Patent Gazette has patent information but does not contain the full patent, only the abstract. The Patent Gazette contains a drawing, the patent number, and one or two paragraphs describing the idea of the invention. If the abstract reveals enough pertinence to warrant reviewing the full patent, you should then go to a depository.

The latest choice is to use the Internet. Go to http://www.USPTO.gov and follow the instructions. It's an on-line version of the Gazette although it has additional information. It's set up so you can read the entire patent and look at the drawings but you can only download and print the abstracts. If you want the whole patent you still must pay for it.

Another alternative to going to the depository is to request copies of the desired patent by writing to the Commissioner of Patent and Trademarks, Box 9, Washington, DC 20231. Have the patent number ready when making this call. There is a charge of $3 for each patent, which is mailed, or $6 for a faxed overnight copy.

Patent Particulars

1. Patents are not renewable! At the end of a patent's period of activity it becomes public domain, thereby making it accessible to and usable by anybody. Do not confuse maintenance with renewable!

If you have new improvements, etc., the day after your patent expires you can file a new patent. You can file a new patent the day after you are granted the first patent. The government does not show favoritism or preferential treatment to a previously patented individual.

2. You may file for a patent only on something that you conceived and/or invented. If it was somebody else's idea, whether they have decided to file for a patent or not, you cannot file for one yourself. The idea belongs to the other person, and you have no rights or claims to a patent.

3. A company or a business cannot be granted a patent. If while working for a company and during that employment you develop a patent, the company can file the paperwork in your name and pay the associated fees. When the patent is granted, you would then assign the company you are working for the rights to that patent.

4. If you plan to file for a foreign patent, you should make the application prior to going public. If you go public before you file, you lose all rights to foreign patents. This is where the Provisional Patent has its value.

5. The USPTO gives you the ability to test market your invention before you invest the time money and effort to obtain patent status. What they allow is a one-year period from the time you go public with your invention to file an application. Here are the particulars:

    The public test period does not commence until you have gone public. Once the invention has been released to the public, you have one calendar year to test it for marketability and decide if you want to proceed with a patent application.

    If during the one-year period you discover that your invention is not saleable or you decide, for whatever reason, to forgo the formality of the patent process, the invention will automatically become public domain one year and one day after the public disclosure.

    Once the invention becomes a matter of public domain, all rights are forgone and nobody, including you, can ever apply for patent protection on the item.

Patent Rights

What rights are granted and what are not? Most people, including those who already have a patent do not understand what rights they have under the law.

1. First of all, until the day you receive a patent number from the USPTO, you have NO RIGHTS at all.

2. What this means is that Registered with the US Patent and Trademark Office, patent applied for, and patent pending mean absolutely nothing other than to provide fair warning to others that someday you MIGHT

have a patent and at that time, and not until then, you will be able to pursue legal action for potential infringement of your patent rights.

3. When you file your patent documentation, the information is registered with the USPTO. However, you are not allowed, under federal statute, to put Registered with the US Patent Office on your product. Products or ideas that have not been officially submitted for patent application are technically prohibited from using this statement.

4. The USPTO does not recognize (or authorize) patent applied for. This is typically a marketing tactic.

5. The USPTO gives patent pending status prior to the issuing of the patent number. The period of time between the granting of patent pending and the patent number is very short.

6. What is granted when a patent is issued is, in the exact language of the statute, the right to exclude others from making, using, or selling the invention.

7. It is up to the inventor to seek out infringement and attempt to halt the manufacture, distribution, and sale of the item that the inventor thinks infringes upon the patent rights.

8. In plain language, if patent infringement occurs, hire an attorney, file suit, and hope that you win before your money runs out!

9. During the period of litigation, there is no guarantee that the courts will grant an injunction against the plaintiff restricting manufacturing and selling, since it's an opinion as to whether or not the inventor's rights are being violated. In the meantime, both parties may elect to continue manufacturing and marketing while the suit is being decided.

Costs of a Patent

"The average cost of filing a patent is $15,000 to $20,000."
The Industry Standard magazine
May 8, 2000

The legal fees associated with preparing and filing a patent application will vary greatly with, for example:

- The complexity of the technology.

- The quality of the write-up and drawings that the inventor can provide.

- The patent attorney's education, experience, and geographic location.

- The number of changes that the inventor makes along the way.

Legal fees in the range of $5,000 to $15,000 for preparation and filing of moderately complex patent applications in technologies such as electronics, computer software, and biotechnology are not uncommon. Check the latest filing fees at http://www.USPTO.gov.

Do you have the ability, both from a business and financial standpoint, to defend the patent, if and when it's granted?

Once a patent has been issued, you are given the right, under the law, to pursue litigation against those parties who you believe are infringing on your rights. Note carefully that patent attorneys are very expensive and the cost of initiating and pursuing legal redress is both expensive and time consuming.

> *". . . an inventor is often forced to go through a long, expensive court process that can easily cost more than US$1 million."*
>
> *"Patent litigation is probably the most expensive form of litigation today."*
>
> Brian Courtney, Chairman and CEO, PEARL

According to the latest statistics, patent infringement violation lawsuits is now the most expensive in the world. Why do you want to spend the time and money to pursue a patent violation? Will you be able to recover the costs of the legal staff and courts, the time you invested in pursuing the legal remedies, and the grief and aggravation involved with the entire process?

Here's the summary of this item—if you can afford the patent but cannot afford the defense of the patent, it's worthless to you as a protectable entity. It's sort of like being able to afford a gun but not the bullets; superficially, it looks dangerous but when it comes time to perform as a true self-defense weapon, it's worthless.

I had an experience several years ago with an elderly couple that had mortgaged their home to finance a patent. After I asked this question, the couple realized that they had expended all of their resources to obtain the patent and couldn't afford to defend it if somebody decided to steal their idea.

Another problem arises when it comes time to find those who are infringing your patent rights. How will you know? Suppose you live in California and have a patent on a product. You've building and marketing the product and are making enough money with it to make it worth your while.

A firm in some Eastern state, North Carolina for example, decides to use your patent and produces a product that is clearly a violation of your rights. The problem is that they're only producing a small quantity of products and you'll never know it because they're only selling in their area and the word never gets to you. Even if you do find out, there's also the matter of the low dollar volume that they're doing which makes it impractical for you to pursue legal action even though you're entitled to do it.

Do You Really Want A Patent?

As an inventor, have you considered this question when considering whether or not you want or even need a patent?

Part of the frustration that invades the invention community is the concept that you must have a patent in place before you even attempt to determine the marketability. The problems involved with patenting are so severe that this premise alone prevents many inventors from ever entering the marketplace.

What follows are three very focused and practical questions that you need to consider when you're looking at the realities of the patent process.

I've addressed several inventors' workshops and support groups and almost always find them to be overly concerned with the patent process. So much so that the members create an atmosphere of paranoia about having to get a patent before they make any progressive moves or decisions.

Don't operate on someone else's agenda and let them tell you what you should do, must do, or ought to do in order to be successful. The world is filled with people who will be happy to give you advice as to what you need to do to be successful. In most cases, they have never done anything that even resembles getting a patent, let alone, marketing an idea, so their comments are virtually worthless.

Anyhow, here are the questions for your consideration:

1. Is there any real advantage to having a patent? Remember that patenting gives you the right to sue someone that you believe is violating your rights. The financial and business issues surrounding the process are expensive and time consuming. If you're an industry leader, and making money with your patented products, you might find it beneficial to pursue patent violations.

   On the other hand, if you're not making much money or none at all with your inventions, patented or not, pursuing legal remedies is a loss both financially and time wise.

   Another critical question is whether or not the industry you have chosen to invent for needs, or even wants, you to have a patent. Sears currently has a mandate that says they will not look at or consider anything that has not been patented. Conversely, I spent several years in the toy business where I was involved with licensing millions of dollars worth of toys from independent inventors and we had no interest in patents.

The time involved in patenting must be considered too. The toy business is a fashion business and the products change very rapidly. Even though there are toys and games that are patentable, very few products in the industry are ever patented because it takes too long to get a patent. The industry calculates (and correctly) that the market for the product will probably have come and gone by the time the patent is issued and production, marketing, and manufacturing is in place.

2. Can someone else come along and create a derivative idea, based on yours, and go to market with a competing item anyway? Once you obtain a patent, the full disclosure of what you've done, how you've done it, and all of the drawings to accompany it are available for everybody to see and review.

With the Internet access at http://www.USPTO.gov so readily available, it's even easier for others to review your creations. Individuals and organizations that feel there is a financial reward connected with exploiting your invention, or something similar to it, will have immediate access to all of your designs and specifications to use as a foundation for creating their own design that does the same thing but doesn't infringe on your patent.

Here's a true story: Liquid Paper was the brainchild of a quick-thinking woman with poor typing skills. Bette Nesmith Graham, the mother of The Monkees' Michael Nesmith, in an effort to cover her typing mistakes, decided to do what painters did when they made mistakes—she painted over them. With a bottle of white paint and a watercolor brush, Graham started on the road to fame and fortune as the inventor of Liquid Paper.

By 1976, the company employed 200 people, made 25 million bottles of Liquid Paper and distributed the product to 31 countries. Graham sold the company four years later to Gillette Corporation for $47.5 million.

That's the good news—the bad news is that because the product was patented, the formula was publicly available and several other firms quickly discovered a variety of ways to accomplish the same thing but without violating the patent. Remember Sno-Paque? It was a legal knock off of Liquid Paper!

Even though the dollar amount in this example was significant enough for most of us to say, "Who cares?" not all products reach this level of success before they get knocked off.

3. Is what you're claiming for patent rights what gives the product value? This is one that always gets inventors upset and cranky. Please note that the question is NOT about the value of the overall invention but whether or not the portion of the invention that a patent attorney tells you is patentable is what makes people want to buy it.

Any patent attorney will tell you that if your invention is complicated enough, there is likely to be one or more components that are a candidate for patenting. The problem is that the patentable component may be so insignificant that nobody cares about it and even if they do, there may be a non-infringing way to get around the problem.

For example, let's say that you've invented a new riveting device and the mounting system that you use to attach it to a table is patentable. Keep in mind that the device itself, which is useful and practical, is not patentable but is highly marketable.

Another firm discovers that you're making money with your invention and decides to make one of their own to compete with you. They discover, by researching the patent archives, that the only part of your invention that's patented is the mounting system.

They can elect to either design their own mounting system or copy one that's public domain and go to market in competition with you and since they're not violating your patent rights you cannot sue them.

The other side of the question has to do with the consumer's perception of the value of patenting. Just think about this: as a consumer, have you ever:

- Purchased a product because of a patent number?

- Having purchased the product, gone down to the patent library and researched what the patent number is?

- Purchased a product with patent applied for or patent pending and after a few years, sent the product back to get the real thing?

As consumers, we have very little respect or use for patents. There are some manufacturers that deal only with patented products. There are still other manufacturers (and a growing number) that do not require patents before manufacturing. Different industries have different requirements.

Recommendations

Patentability, marketability, and profitability are mutually exclusive concepts. However, patents can be both valuable and useful if you apply them properly. Here's the recommended procedure for pursuing both the marketability and patentability of your inventions:

- File a Provisional Patent with the USPTO.

- Have a novelty search performed by a patent attorney.

- If the novelty search reveals that you're not violating anyone else's patent and that you're probably a candidate a patent, perform the solicitation and market research tasks.

- If you discover that you cannot find a buyer or licensee for your invention, do NOT pursue a patent.

- If you discover that a buyer or licensee does not want or require a patent to obtain the rights from you (the toy industry), do not pursue a patent.

- If you find a buyer or licensee who is seriously interested and requires that your invention be patented, pursue the patent.

Chapter 6
Trademarks and
Copyrights

**1,500 trademarks are encountered daily (estimate)
30,000 in a supermarket**

Trademarks

Because of the amount of advertising, promotion, publicity, and subsequent reputation that becomes connected with goods and services, trademarks tend to become the identity under which people recognize and purchase a particular line of goods or services from a supplier.

In other words, a trademark is the mark of your trade or how your goods and services come to be known and recognized. As a result, the trademark may become as valuable, or even more valuable, than the goods or services, which it represents.

The clutter dude and name *Clutterology*® shown at the right is an example of a registered trademark. They belong to Nancy Miller, the owner and creator of the book and training program *Clutterology*® *Getting Rid of Clutter and Getting Organized* and she, and she alone, can use these marks or authorize others to use them.

***Clutterology*®**

Incidentally, the registered mark includes the graphic character clutter dude the name (Clutterology), or both when they are used together.

So what are trademarks? From a practical standpoint they are a word, symbol, slogan, or even a distinctive sound, which identifies and distinguishes the goods and services of one party from those of another. Some specifics of trademarks are that they:

- Take 6 to 13 months to be granted depending on the category selected and the backlog of work.

- Are granted for a period of 10 years and are renewable, as long as the mark is maintained in an active status.

- Have maintenance fees. If the forms are not filed and the fees are not paid, the mark is considered to have been abandoned or canceled, and deprives the registrant of the exclusive right to use the mark.

- Cost $375 per submission, not including charges for the artwork, forms, etc.

- Require the filing of a form and payment between the 5th and 6th year in order to ensure they do not fall into the public domain.

- Are considered to be an asset and may be bought, sold, leased, licensed, traded, bartered, confiscated, awarded, or willed in any form of sale, legal action, trust, or judgment.

- Have 34 classes of goods and 8 classes of services under which a trademark may be registered. It is possible to register the same name in different classes of goods or services.

- May be done if either the name or the graphic portion of the trademark is deceptively similar to another trademark in the same category.

Mr. Peanut was first used in 1916
Mr. Peanut trademark was registered in 1925

Filing a Trademark

In order to prevent the rejection of a trademark application, you are encouraged to research trademarks that are in existence at the time of application.

The process involves six primary steps:

1. You can do a manual submission using the US Government forms. To obtain them, write using a postcard that includes your name and address in the upper left-hand corner on the front and address it to:

US Department of Commerce
Patent and Trademark Office
Washington DC 20231

On the back of the postcard write:

"Please send me a copy of the *Basic Information Concerning Trademarks.*"

or you can go to http://www.USPTO.gov and obtain your materials on-line using the Internet.

2. Review the book, *Basic Information Concerning Trademarks,* as it shows you exactly how to develop the artwork, how to fill out the forms, and how to submit them. It'll also provide you with a current list of product and service classifications so you'll know which category applies to your trademark.

3. Design the graphic logo and determine the name or slogan.

4. Have a preliminary trademark search run to determine if the mark you want to register is available or has already been taken.

   A preliminary search can be run by a patent agent, patent attorney or the patent and trademark room of a patent library to determine if the mark is available or taken.

   You'll find that many of the public libraries offer the trademark search service for a minimal fee. Some public libraries will perform the research, by computer, for $50 to $100, depending on the amount of on-line computer time required. It usually includes a search of federal and state trademarks.

   The federal search is inclusive from 1884 to within a few weeks of the present and is updated on a weekly basis. The file does not include those marks that were canceled (an affidavit was not filed in the fifth or sixth year), abandoned (the trademark was never published) or expired (the trademark was not renewed).

5. Place the mark, name, slogan, etc. on a product and make a legitimate sale of the product, across state lines, in exchange for money. It's mandatory that you sell a product with the mark affixed. This is defined as using the mark in commerce, and is a requirement for receiving a trademark.

   By strict definition, one usage of the mark is all that is required to comply with the letter of the law. Selling a single item with the mark affixed across state lines (interstate commerce) fulfills the requirements.

6. File the completed application, artwork, etc. with the USPTO. You'll need to provide the USPTO with five samples of the mark as it's used. A supply of samples of the mark, logo, package, letterhead, etc., will suffice.

Do not send the product!

Trademark Marks

The marks (™, ℠, and ®) indicate different things:

1. The ™ (trademark) may be placed on any logo, name, slogan, etc., as fair warning to others that you are using this as your trademark.

2. The ℠ (service mark) is usually placed on a logo or other device for firms that are dealing with a service, rather than a product. The rights, restrictions, and cautions are the same as when using the ™.

3. The ® (registered mark) is allowed on a mark only after the mark has been officially approved and granted by the USPTO.

The, ™, ℠ or ® marking should be large enough to be easily spotted and should be placed as either a superscript (shoulder) or subscript (heel) immediately following the mark.

You can check the latest filing fees at http://www.USPTO.gov. Look under "file" and then "Filing Fee and Refund Policy" to see what's new.

The Monopoly trademark was registered in 1935.

Infringement

Some of the more important rights accorded to a trademark holder are as follows:

1. The right to sue in federal court for trademark infringements.

2. Recovery of profits, damages, and costs in a federal court infringement action and the possibility of treble damages and attorneys fees.

3. Constructive notice of a claim of ownership.

4. Upon presentation of prima facie evidence of valid ownership of the mark, the exclusive rights to the usage of the mark as defined in the registration.

5. Availability of criminal penalties in an action for counterfeiting a registered trademark.

6. Providing a basis for filing trademark applications in foreign countries.

The trademark laws define trademark violations as being violations of the counterfeiting laws since they are a form of forgery or counterfeiting.

Deceptively Similar

A mark may be denied if it is declared to be deceptively similar to an existing name or mark. It is the mark, which identifies and distinguishes the goods and services of one party from those of another.

Let's look at an example. Let's say that you have decided to market a line of batteries in the US but you're going to have them manufactured in the Philippines. You know that the name Duracell (a registered trademark of Mallory) and the black and copper coloring (trade dress) are what people use as a guideline for selecting the batteries for their electronic equipment.

You decide to call your batteries Durable Cell and make the coloring on your batteries black and brown.

From a distance, or at a quick glance, the customer might confuse your batteries with the Duracell line because the names are similar and the coloring or trade dress is close enough to be confusing.

Because the customer might confuse the two brands, the mark will probably be denied especially, if it appears that the sole reason for the similarity is to confuse the customer into believing that they are buying the other trademarked item.

Trademark Graveyard

There is a caution or drawback regarding trademarks. A manufacturer spends considerable advertising dollars to get the name of the product in front of the consumer. If the consumers begin to use the trademark name generically, the government can withdraw the trademark. There have been numerous occurrences in our past: aspirin, elevator, kerosene, octane and even linoleum, just to name a few.

Trademarks and the Internet

If you own a trademark and find that someone is holding it hostage as a domain name until you pay a large sum for it, you may be the victim of cybersquatting. You can either sue to get your domain name—and possibly some money damages—under a 1999 federal law known as the Anti-Cybersquatting Consumer Protection Act, or you can initiate arbitration proceedings under the authority of the Internet Corporation of Assigned Names and Numbers (ICANN) and win the name back without the expense and aggravation of a lawsuit.

Cybersquatting means registering, selling or using a domain name with the intent of profiting from the goodwill of someone else's trademark. It generally refers to the practice of buying up domain names that use the names of existing businesses with the intent to sell the names for a profit to those businesses.

The practice that's come to be known as cybersquatting originated at a time when most businesses were not savvy about the commercial opportunities on the Internet. Some entrepreneurial souls registered the names of well-known companies as domain names, with the intent of selling the names back to the companies when they finally woke up. Panasonic, Fry's Electronics, Hertz and Avon were among the "victims" of cybersquatters. Opportunities for cybersquatters are rapidly diminishing, because most businesses now know that nailing down domain names is a high priority.

How do you know if the domain name you want is being used by a cybersquatter? As a general rule, first check to see if the domain name takes you to a legitimate website. If the domain name takes you to a website that appears to be functional and reasonably related in its subject matter to the domain name, you probably aren't facing a case of cybersquatting. However, you may have a case of trademark infringement. If your browser produces any of the following results:

- You get a "can't find server" message.

- You get an "under construction" page, or

- You get a page that appears to have no relationship to the meaning of the domain name.

Although each of these results suggests the possibility of cybersquatting, there may also be an innocent explanation, especially if the website is still under construction. You can reserve a domain name for two years, so the fact that a website is not up and running, even months after the name was reserved or registered, does not necessarily mean that the registrant doesn't have perfectly legitimate plans to have a website in the future.

Before jumping to any conclusions, contact the domain name registrant. To find the name and address of a domain name owner, you can use the "WHOIS Lookup" at http://www.whois.net. Find out whether there is a reasonable explanation for the use of the domain name, or if the registrant is willing to sell you the name at a price you are willing to pay.

Sometimes, you may find that paying the cybersquatter is the easiest choice. It may be a lot cheaper and quicker for you to come to terms with a squatter than to file a lawsuit or initiate an arbitration hearing: these processes cost money, and although you may be able to recover your costs and attorney fees if you win, there is no guarantee; it's completely up to the judge.

A victim of cybersquatting in the United States can now sue under the provisions of the Anti-cybersquatting Consumer Protection Act (ACPA) or can fight the cybersquatter using ICANN. The ACPA defines cybersquatting as registering, trafficking in or using a domain name with the intent to profit in bad faith from the goodwill of a trademark belonging to someone else. The

ICANN arbitration system is considered by trademark experts to be faster and less expensive than suing under the ACPA, and the procedure does not require an attorney.

The ACPA authorizes a trademark owner to sue an alleged cybersquatter in federal court and obtain a court order transferring the domain name back to the trademark owner. In some cases, the cybersquatter must pay money damages.

In order to stop a cybersquatter, the trademark owner must prove all of the following:

- The domain name registrant had a bad-faith intent to profit from the trademark.

- The trademark was distinctive at the time the domain name was first registered.

- The domain name is identical or confusingly similar to the trademark, and

- The trademark qualifies for protection under federal trademark laws— that is, the trademark is distinctive and its owner was the first to use the trademark in commerce.

If the person or company who registered the domain name had reasonable grounds to believe that the use of the domain name was fair and lawful, they can avoid a court decision that they acted in bad faith. In other words, if the accused cybersquatter can show a judge that he had a reason to register the domain name other than to sell it back to the trademark owner for a profit, then a court will probably allow him to keep the domain name.

In 1999, after assuming control of domain name registration, ICANN adopted and began implementing the Uniform Domain Name Dispute Resolution Policy (UDNDRP) a policy for resolution of domain name disputes. This international policy results in an arbitration of the dispute, not litigation. An action can be brought by any person who complains (referred to by ICANN as the "complainant") that:

- A domain name is identical or confusingly similar to a trademark or service mark in which the complainant has rights.

- The domain name owner has no rights or legitimate interests in the domain name, and

- The domain name has been registered and is being used in bad faith.

All of these elements must be established in order for the complainant to prevail. If the complainant prevails, the domain name will be canceled or transferred to the complainant, but financial remedies are not available under the UDNDRP. Information about initiating a complaint is provided at the ICANN website.

Also, don't assume that you have the right to use your own name or company name to identify your product. You don't if the name is already a registered mark. Even Senator Exxon (Mr. Decency himself) couldn't open up a gas station with his own name on it.

Final suggestion: never use a product or service name until you check to see if the name is already registered.

This area of the law can get quite tricky. Although the forms appear simple, there is more to it than meets the eye. We strongly suggest you consult with an attorney to protect what might be your most valuable asset.

Copyrights

Wouldn't you know it, the most powerful form of protection available is both the cheapest and the easiest to obtain? It's called copyright and it gives the creator of original works of authorship the exclusive rights to make copies or to authorize others to make copies.

Copyrights are technically defined as original works of authorship including literary, dramatic, musical, artistic, and certain other intellectual works. They're automatically granted upon the fixing (creation) of an idea in fixed or tangible form.

Copyright is a form of protection provided by the laws of the US (title 17, US Code) to the authors of original works. This protection is available to both published and unpublished works.

Section 106 of the 1976 Copyright Act generally gives the owner of copyright the exclusive right to do and to authorize others to do the following:

• To reproduce the work in copies or phonorecords;

• To prepare derivative works based upon the work;

• To distribute copies or phonorecords of the work to the public by sale or other transfer of ownership, or by rental, lease, or lending;

• To perform the work publicly, in the case of literary, musical, dramatic, and choreographic works, pantomimes, and motion pictures and other audiovisual works;

• To display the copyrighted work publicly, in the case of literary, musical, dramatic, and choreographic works, pantomimes, and pictorial, graphic, or sculptural works, including the individual images of a motion picture or other audiovisual work; and

- In the case of sound recordings, to perform the work publicly by means of a digital audio transmission.

If the word phonorecords is unfamiliar to you, original copyright laws were intended to cover the old vinyl records as the sole means of storing sound. The term has since come to mean virtually any form of recording device or medium that allows the faithful recording and replaying of material, either audible, visible, digital, or a combination of them.

It is illegal for anyone to violate any of the rights provided by the copyright law to the owner of copyright. These rights, however, are not unlimited in scope. Sections 107 through 121 of the 1976 Copyright Act establish limitations on these rights.

In some cases, these limitations are specified exemptions from copyright liability. One major limitation is the doctrine of fair use, which is given a statutory basis in Section 107 of the 1976 Copyright Act.

In other instances, the limitation takes the form of a compulsory license under which certain limited uses of copyrighted works are permitted upon payment of specified royalties and compliance with statutory conditions.

For further information about the limitations of any of these rights, consult the copyright law or write to the Copyright Office (http://www.LOC.gov).

Securing A Copyright

The way in which copyright protection is secured is frequently misunderstood. No publication, registration or other action in the Copyright Office is required to secure copyright. There are, however, certain definite advantages to registration.

Copyright is secured automatically when the work is created, and a work is created when it is fixed in a copy or phonorecord for the first time. Copies are material objects from which a work can be read or visually perceived either directly or with the aid of a machine or device, such as books, manuscripts, sheet music, film, videotape, or microfilm. Phonorecords are material objects embodying fixations of sounds (excluding, by statutory definition, motion picture soundtracks), such as cassette tapes, CDs, or LPs. Thus, for example, a song (the work) can be fixed in sheet music (copies) or in phonograph disks (phonorecords), or both.

How long do copyrights last?

The answer currently is the life of the author plus 80 years.

Of course, for purposes of registering your latest innovations, the latest laws apply, but if you are concerned about possible infringement of something that has already been copyrighted, then you'll need to take a look at what's happened in the past and how long that protection stays in effect.

- Works originally created on or after January 1, 1978. A work that is created (fixed in tangible form for the first time) on or after January 1, 1978, is automatically protected from the moment of its creation and is ordinarily given a term enduring for the author's life plus an additional 80 years after the author's death. In the case of "a joint work prepared by two or more authors who did not work-for-hire," the term lasts for 80 years after the last surviving author's death. For works-made-for-hire, and for anonymous and pseudonymous works (unless the author's identity is revealed in Copyright Office records), the duration of copyright will be 95 years from publication or 120 years from creation, whichever is shorter.

- Works originally created before January 1, 1978, but not published or registered by that date. These works have been automatically brought under the statute and are now given federal copyright protection. The duration of copyright in these works will generally be computed in the same way as for works created on or after January 1, 1978: the life-plus 80 or 95/120-year terms will apply to them as well. The law provides that in no case will the term of copyright for works in this category expire before December 31, 2002, and for works published on or before December 31, 2002, the term of copyright will not expire before December 31, 2047.

- Works originally created and published or registered before January 1, 1978. Under the law in effect before 1978, copyright was secured either on the date a work was published with a copyright notice or on the date of registration if the work was registered in unpublished form. In either case, the copyright endured for a first term of 28 years from the date it was secured. During the last (28th) year of the first term, the copyright was eligible for renewal. The Copyright Act of 1976 extended the renewal term from 28 to 47 years for copyrights that were subsisting on January 1, 1978, or for pre-1978 copyrights restored under the Uruguay Round Agreements Act (URAA), making these works eligible for a total term of protection of 75 years.

- Public Law 105-298, enacted on October 27, 1998, further extended the renewal term of copyrights still subsisting on that date by an additional 20 years, providing for a renewal term of 67 years and a total term of protection of 95 years.

- Public Law 102-307, enacted on June 26, 1992, amended the 1976 Copyright Act to provide for automatic renewal of the term of copyrights secured between January 1, 1964, and December 31, 1977. Although the renewal term is automatically provided, the Copyright Office does not issue a renewal certificate for these works unless a renewal application and fee are received and registered in the Copyright Office.

- Public Law 102-307 makes renewal registration optional. Thus, filing for renewal registration is no longer required in order to extend the original 28-year copyright term to the full 95 years. However, some benefits accrue from making a renewal registration during the 28th year of the original term.

Copyrights can be registered with the government (although there are other ways to do it), cost a mere $45 filing fee for each application, and the protection is available to both published and unpublished (not yet released to the world at large) works.

You can get all the information you need to file your own copyrights, including the forms, from the Library of Congress at http://www.loc.gov/copyright/. In addition, http://www.benedict.com is a support website that has a wealth of information, forms, and services that will assist you in the copyright process.

What Rights Are Cover or Protected?

Copyright protects original works of authorship that are fixed in a tangible form of expression. The fixation need not be directly perceptible so long as it may be communicated with the aid of a machine or device. Copyrightable works include the following categories:

1. Literary works. Literary copyrights are the most familiar for many of us. Look for the copyright notice whenever you open a book. It's usually listed on the backside of the title page or at the bottom of handouts or on brochures in the margins.

2. Musical works, including any accompanying words. This includes MP3, compact disc, cassette tapes, and phonographic records. Everything from music-on-hold, elevator music, music in the malls, radio stations and even music in the gym is policed primarily by two organizations, ASCAP (American Society of Composers, Authors and Publishers http://www.ascap.com) and BMI (Broadcast Music Incorporated http://www.BMI.com). BMI operates as a not-for-profit organization. They represent more than 180,000 songwriters, composers, and music publishers with 3,000,000 works in all areas of music. BMI distributes royalties to its songwriters, computers, and publishers, for the public performance and digital home copying of their works. BMI keeps track of local radio broadcasting, noncommercial college radio, and television feature, theme and cue music performed on networks, cable TV stations and local TV stations.

3. Dramatic works, including any accompanying music. This category includes scripts, stage plays, poetry, operas, and related works of an artistic nature. It includes dramatic works, including any accompanying words, like plays and screenplays. Most professional screenwriters and playwrights always file copyright on their work before exposing it to the public.

4. Pantomimes and choreographic works. These works include the dance routines for major theatrical productions like Cats, A Chorus Line, Les Misérables, the routines of mimes, cheerleader routines, or the Radio

City Music Hall Rockettes Dancers. This category also includes football and basketball play books where the moves and actions of the teams are pre-organized or choreographed by the coach for the sole and exclusive usage of the team they coach. For a team member or other person to copy and distribute those plans is a violation of the copyright laws and makes the person who copies the material liable for both civil and criminal prosecution. The dance step *The Electric Slide* is a registered dance pattern.

5. Pictorial, graphic, and sculptural works. This category includes photographs, cartoon characters, and maps. Other familiar items that are covered under this section of copyright include plush dolls (known as soft sculptures), advertising banners and posters. For example, computer programs and most compilations are registered literary works, whereas maps are registered as pictorial, graphic and sculptural works.

6. Motion pictures and other audiovisual works. Audiovisual works include videotapes, DVD's and motion pictures. Motion pictures are audiovisual works consisting of a series of related images which, when shown in succession, impart an impression of motion, together with any accompanying sounds. They are typically embodied in film, videotape, or videodisk. A number of individuals contribute authorship to a motion picture, including the writer, director, producer, camera operator, editors, and others. Sometimes they are jointly listed as the creators of the copyrighted work and sometimes they are not. The reason that all the individuals involved in creating one of these works may not be listed on the copyright as authors is because a motion picture or video production is frequently Work-Made-For-Hire.

7. Sound and video recordings include live, unedited tape or camcorder recordings. This has been greatly expanded to include film, digital pictures, and MP3 recordings. As new methods of recording and playback are developed, they will, by their very nature, be included under this heading.

8. Architectural works. Architectural works are defined as such works as blueprints. An original design of a building embodied in any tangible medium of expression, including building, architectural plans or drawings are protected under copyright law. The work includes the overall form as well as the arrangement and composition of spaces and elements in the design but does not include individual standard features or design elements that are functionally required. For example, a building is a structure that is habitable by humans. It is intended to be both permanent and stationary, such as houses, office buildings, churches, museums, gazebos, and garden pavilions. It's look and the design components that go into it are copyrightable materials.

These categories should be viewed broadly. For example, computer programs and most compilations may be registered as literary works; maps and architectural plans may be registered as pictorial, graphic, and sculptural works.

Not Protected by Copyright

Several categories of material are generally not eligible for federal copyright protection. These include among others:

- Works that have not been fixed in a tangible form of expression (for example, choreographic works that have not been notated or recorded, or improvisational speeches or performances that have not been written or recorded).

- Titles, names, short phrases, and slogans; familiar symbols or designs; mere variations of typographic ornamentation, lettering, or coloring; mere listings of ingredients or contents.

- Ideas, procedures, methods, systems, processes, concepts, principles, discoveries, or devices, as distinguished from a description, explanation, or illustration.

- Works consisting entirely of information that is common property and containing no original authorship (for example: standard calendars, height and weight charts, tape measures and rulers, and lists or tables taken from public documents or other common sources).

Infringement

Like trademark violations, copyright infringement is a form of forgery, the theft and/or usage of someone else's property.

The general principles are as follows:

1. Mere ownership of a book, manuscript, painting, or any other copy does not give the possessor the copyright.

2. The law provides that transfer of ownership of any material object that embodies a protected work does not of itself convey any rights in the copyright.

3. The owner of copyrighted material may make archive copies of the copyrighted material for personal usage. These copies may not be loaned, sold, distributed, rented, or otherwise transmitted to any person or company other than the owner of the copyrighted material. If the copyrighted material is sold or transferred, all archival copies must accompany the copyrighted (original) material.

Case law in this area is pretty scant because of the economic realities of litigation. Copyright infringement doesn't usually become an issue until someone has made some serious money off someone else's creation.

Derivative Work

Because copyright is granted to the author of original works of authorship, it's important that any research work you do prior to actually embarking on what you consider to be original work, be approached judiciously.

If you aren't careful, the work you do may be construed as derivative work, and declared to be the property of the original copyrighted work from which you obtained your inspiration. Only the author, or those deriving their rights through the author, can rightfully claim copyright.

The following examples show some of the many different types of derivative works:

• Television drama (based on a novel).

• Motion picture (based on a play).

• Novel in English (a translation of a book originally published in Russian).

• Drawing (based on a photograph).

• Books of maps (based on public domain maps with some new maps).

• Lithograph (based on a painting).

• Drama about John Doe (based on the letters and journal entries of John Doe).

Copyright Notice Elements

© 2005 Mike Rounds All Right Reserved

A copyright has four elements. They are:

1. The term copyright. The © (c in a circle) notice is used only on visually perceptible copies. Certain kinds of works—for example, musical, dramatic, and literary works—may be fixed not in copies but by means of sound in an audio recording. Since audio recordings such as audiotapes and phonograph disk are phonorecords and not copies, the © (c in a circle) notice is not used to indicate protection of the underlying musical, dramatic, or literary work that is recorded.

2. The year of copyright. This is the year of publication.

3. The name of the copyright holder. The legal owner of the copyright is not necessarily the author or creator of the work. Works created by

employees in the course of their employment or independent workers who sign Work-for-hire Agreements are considered to be creating the work on behalf of the employer. In these works the copyright is vested in the person doing the hiring.

4. And the phrase *All Rights Reserved.*

Fair Use

Fair use provisions of the copyright law allow for limited copying or distribution of published works without the author's permission in some cases. Examples of fair use of copyrighted materials include quotation of excerpts in a review or critique, or copying a small part of a work by a teacher or student to illustrate a lesson. New issues about fair use have arisen with the increased use of the Internet.

Fair use is determined by:

1. The purpose and character of the use, including whether such use is of a commercial nature or is for nonprofit educational purposes.

2. The nature of the copyrighted work.

3. The amount and substantiality of the portion used in relation to the copyrighted work as a whole.

4. The effect of the use upon the potential market for or value of the copyrighted work.

Generally speaking, quotes are considered fair use when less than 250 words are used from one source, like a book or feature length article. Short nonfiction pieces, poems, and songs are different because of their length and you should request permission regardless of how much you use.

Work-Made-For-Hire

Although the general rule is that the person who creates a work is the author of that work, there is an exception. The copyright law defines a category of works called Work-Made-For-Hire. If a work is made-for-hire, the employer and not the employee is considered the author. The employer may be a firm or organization or an individual.

Section 101 of the copyright law defines Work-Made-For-Hire as:

1. A work prepared by an employee within the scope of his or her employment; or

2. A work specially ordered or commissioned for use as a contribution to a collective work, as a part of a motion picture or other audiovisual work, as a translation, as a supplementary work, as a compilation, as an instructional text, as a test, as answer material for a test, as an atlas, if

the parties expressly agree in a written instrument signed by them that the work shall be considered a Work-Made-For-Hire.

Examples of works for hire created in an employment relationship are:

- A software program created by a staff programmer for a computer company.

- A newspaper article written by a staff journalist for publication in a daily newspaper.

- A musical arrangement written for XYZ Music Company by a salaried arranger on its staff.

Filing a Copyright

To register a work, send the following three elements in the same envelope or package to:

> Library of Congress
> Copyright Office
> 101 Independence Ave SE
> Washington DC 20559-6000

1. A properly completed application form (http://www.loc.gov).

2. A non-refundable filing fee of $45 for each application.

    Note: Copyright Office fees are subject to change. For current fees, please check the Copyright Office web site at http://www.loc.gov/copyright, write the Copyright Office, or call 202-707-3000.

3. Non-returnable deposit of the work being registered. The deposit requirements vary in particular situations. The general requirements follow. Also note the information under Special Deposit Requirements.

    a. If the work was first published in the US on or after January 1, 1978, two complete copies or phonorecords of the best edition.

    b. If the work was first published in the US before January 1, 1978, two complete copies or phonorecords of the work as first published.

    c. If the work was first published outside the US, one complete copy or phonorecord of the work as first published.

    d. If sending multiple works, all applications, deposits, and fees should be sent in the same package. If possible, applications should be attached to the appropriate deposit. Whenever possible, number each package (e. g., 1 of 3, 2 of 4) to facilitate processing.

Chapter 7
Are You Market Ready?

Even though your invention works, it might not be ready for mass manufacturing and distribution. Since most inventions are designed to solve a specific problem, inventors are usually concerned with the specific solution to the problem and not with the bureaucracy surrounding the world of mass marketing.

You are now involved in a two-stage selling effort; sell to (the manufacturers) and sell through (to the consumer). Manufacturers are required to comply with government and other regulatory requirements, live up to media expectations, and generally obey performance standards that someone else has set.

If your target industry has to comply with a standard that you have not complied with, the manufacturer might reject your invention because it doesn't fit the current trends, standards, or requirements.

The list of questions below, which is like a pilot's checklist, should become a part of your basic guidelines during the development phase of your invention.

The questions are designed to get you to think about your product and its readiness for market acceptance. It's not designed for right or wrong answers—just to help get you ready to offer your inventions and have the manufacturer look favorably on your invention.

The recommendation for answering these questions is as follows:

• Go someplace quiet and private where you won't be disturbed.

• If possible, take a trusted friend along to ask you the questions and to carefully review the answers. A FRIEND is defined as someone who will tell you the truth, not what you want to hear.

- This list of questions is designed to get you ready to offer your invention to the public and make a profit. Consequently, you need to know the truth and if there is something that's not quite right, you'll need to fix it before you release it.

Here are the basic considerations for success.

Legal Compliance

Are there legal compliance requirements to be considered?

As citizens, we are governed by criminal laws. In the world of manufacturing and marketing, civil compliance is the order of the day.

Many industries have strong ties to agencies like Underwriters Laboratories, the Food and Drug Administration, and related regulatory bodies that set and monitor standards for performance and other related aspects of the products that are offered to the public. If your invention is determined to be noncompliant, these agencies may block the sale of the invention.

For example, during my days as Director of Engineering with Notifier Corporation, I was responsible for the testing and compliance of millions of smoke detectors. Since smoke detectors are classed as a life saving device, the manufacture and testing are controlled by a tightly regulated set of standards that are imposed by the fire marshals and monitored by UL (Underwriters Laboratories).

Every time we made a change or added an accessory to an existing smoke detector design, we had to resubmit the modification to UL for approval before it was legal for sale.

We were constantly reviewing ideas for new designs, accessories, and products to enhance the line. One of the first considerations was whether the designer was aware of, and in compliance with, the latest laws and regulations that governed the manufacture, test, and sales of smoke detectors.

To make sure that you're in compliance with what the current rules, regulations and laws require for offering your ideas to the public, review the current industry compliance standards while you're perfecting your invention, and take every care to be sure that you are designing with the current guidelines.

If you're not sure where to obtain these standards, go to the library (or the Internet) and locate the trade journals and magazines that address the industry in which you have chosen to invent.

Contact the editors of these magazines and ask them about compliance rules and regulations. In 99 out of 100 cases, they'll know exactly where you need to go to get the information because they're in the business and are constantly writing about compliance requirement.

Safety and Packaging

Are there any safety and/or packaging considerations?

It seems like every time we turn around, there are new standards for child safety; tamper resistance, warning labels, and other ancillary items that have nothing to do with the performance of the product. However, they do have to do with its salability because the manufacturers have to comply with these standards in order to legally offer the item to the public.

As in the previous question, if you're not sure where to obtain these standards, go to the library (or the Internet) and locate the trade journals and magazines that address the industry in which you have chosen to invent.

When I was in the toy business, we were governed by a set of rules called PS 72-76. This was a set of safety and compliance standards that was developed by the Toy Manufacturer's Association (TMA) in conjunction with the Consumer Products Safety Association (CPSA).

This document, that was the size of a phone book, had all of the safety and age grading standards for everything you could think of that was classified as a toy or game. It included very specific standards for things like sharp points, chemical composition of paints, toxicity standards, and hazardous components like small parts that could cause a child to choke.

This standard is the reason why you don't find little *goodies* in Cracker Jacks any more. The small toys could cause a choking hazard in children and were completely eliminated from Cracker Jacks to be in compliance with the safety rules.

According to Dan Poynter, author of *The Self-Publishing Manual*, "Packaging is everything. Each year, corporations spend more than $50 billion on product packaging and design. That's $50 billion—not for the products themselves *or* for the wrapper—but $50 billion just for the *design* of the wrapper."

Packaging is a critical component because it's what the consumer sees first. If it's deceptive, or misleading, it becomes a liability and a potential for a lawsuit at some point in the future.

Some products are just plain difficult to package and this difficulty results in packages that are big, waste space, and antagonize merchants.

Rubic's Cube evolved into another popular puzzle that was pyramid shaped and required a special box to make it square so it would sit on the shelves. This might not sound like a big deal but the square box took almost twice as much room as the product and was not a popular item with retailers because of the wasted space.

Look carefully at what kinds of packaging are going to be required at the different levels of manufacturing and distribution. Make sure that you do your homework during the design stage and develop whatever criterion is required to ensure that the manufacturer does not reject the item because of this concern.

Environmental Considerations

Are there environmental impact considerations or regulatory compliance standards that must be followed?

Here's a proven fact—concern for the environment is growing. Many local, state, and federal agencies have stepped in and have the power to block the manufacturing or distribution of products that pollute or contaminate the environment.

New products that affect the environment negatively will probably not be candidates for acceptance. The concerned cries of the public, as well as the regulatory agency's penalties, make it too cumbersome for most manufacturers to consider negative environmental impact inventions.

Court rulings have not only blocked new products based on the components and materials used in the products, but have also ruled on the negative effects of the manufacturing processes used to create the products.

Also consider that if the manufacturing processes or materials used are detrimental to the environment, your invention might be rejected because of them, even though the product itself is environmentally sound and works great.

On the other hand, do you have a product that is good for the environment? If the answer is yes, then you're looking at a strong collaborator in those who are looking for ways to help clean up the environment.

The marketplace has been peppered with products in the past decade that wouldn't have even been considered before the move to clean up the planet.

It's in your best interest to learn as much as you can about what it's actually going to take to manufacture your invention. Look at being environmentally friendly as a strong asset in your favor and be sure to exploit it whenever you promote your creativity.

Market Potential

Is there a broad potential market for your product or are you targeting a narrow, vertical market?

Neither one is necessarily better than the other, but it's in your best interest to determine who the target market will be. The determination of the market should have a major impact on the materials you choose; the design criteria established as guidelines, and ultimately, the manufacturing methods used.

For example, the early Mazda sports cars had an area in the back for storage. Because it was open, anybody who passed by could look in and see if it was worth their while to break into the car.

One of my students developed a security cover for the back of the Mazda. The cover made the open area look like a floor and hid whatever items were in the back thus providing a security deterrent. If this item seems like a common accessory for today's cars, it wasn't back then. Sometimes when a manufacturer overlooks an item, it provides a great market for an independent inventor.

His target market was an owner of a particular model of Mazda that did not have a security cover. By defining his target market, he made his security cover a much more appealing item for licensing because the potential licensee already knew where the market was, how big it was, and what kind of percentage return they could probably expect once they went to market.

On the other hand, an electric air freshener that will work in any automobile has a broad-based market. It's potential for sales rely on its general appeal to the consumer and the market is very broad rather than a narrow, precisely targeted group.

Knowing what your overall market potential will be is a key factor in a variety of design elements including form factor, shape, color, materials, manufacturing techniques, and overall durability.

Life Cycle

Will the invention have a long enough life cycle with a stable demand, what's the anticipated pay back period, and will the consumer pay a price that's high enough to return the initial investments together with a profit?

The concern is whether the manufacturer believes that there is enough time to develop, market and sell enough units to be profitable. If not, they probably won't consider the invention viable.

Let's be honest about it—this is all about making money with your inventions so you have to know if the lifetime popularity will be long enough to make enough money to make it viable. If it looks like your creations are at the tail end of a popularity cycle or if it's going to be a short-lived market that's currently dominated by firms that have a lock on the marketplace, you might not be able to get your ideas to market in time to capitalize on the current buying trends.

This is becoming a tougher question to analyze and answer with each passing day because of the volatility of today's marketplace. The process revolves around market projection analysis and has as much to do with crystal ball gazing as it does with marketing research and trend analysis.

The first thing to determine is how long products currently last in your target industry. We're living in a world where products are becoming obsolete at a rapid pace. Most items will have less than a five–year life because of innovations.

Each industry has its projected life cycles, and knowing what they are should affect some of the decisions about the design of your product.

Obviously, if the trend looks to be too short to be profitable, the manufacturer may reject the invention. On the other hand, the manufacturer may be an aggressive and risk–taking manufacturer and attempt to beat the timeline.

Your best solution to this dilemma comes from reviewing the current trends and product longevity of your target industry. This should give you a relative indication of how long current and past products have been lasting.

For example, I had a client who had developed a line of great accessories for the Razor scooter. They were wonderful devices, worked well, and had everything going for them except for one thing—they arrived too late to capitalize on the immense popularity of the primary item, the Razor scooter itself.

The products were called the *Hyperscoot,* a steering dampener that allowed the Razor to perform tight turns and make sharp maneuvers without dumping the rider on the ground and the *DitchDigger,* a wheel base extender that allowed the Razor to be ridden on broken terrain and uneven surfaces.

The end result was that although the products had great possibilities, the remaining time left on the marketplace was too short to make them of interest to the firms who were currently servicing the scooter market.

The products are still sitting in the inventor's workshop together with the patent applications, marketing plan, business plan, and other materials that will probably never result in any kind of successful marketing or profitability.

It's not enough to find that an invention fits into your lifestyle or needs—you MUST do market research to determine what's been happening and what the industry is currently seeking in the way of solutions for its concerns and what its done in the past. This is like driving by looking in the rear view mirror, but it's about the best indicator we have.

Just keep in mind that from a developer's standpoint, the more you know, the better off you'll be as you make decisions about timing and development cycles.

Feasibility

Is it functionally and economically feasible?

It's one thing to make your prototype work but it's entirely different to get high volume production at a reasonable price and good quality.

Prototypes are often built with available materials. Those materials may be far too exotic or expensive to be used in mass production yet the performance requirements of the expensive components are what make the product work better than its predecessors.

For example, I was involved with the inventor of a spinning light device in the mid 1980's. It responded to sound and spun the fiber optics in some dramatic patterns. The inventor was brilliant and his application of simple concepts to produce beautiful light patterns dazzled everyone who saw the devices.

He licensed the product to a firm in Los Angeles who had distribution throughout the world plus some wonderful connections with several catalog companies. This combination made the product a potential winner for everyone. The problems started to occur when the prototypes had to be production engineered.

It turned out that the inventor would buy parts from government surplus auctions, often at pennies on the dollar from their market price. His workshop was stocked with lots of parts and pieces he acquired for next to nothing and this formed his basic stock of parts for his new inventions.

The parts that made the lighting system work so well were dependant on some slick little motors that he bought for about 10 cents apiece. The problem was that the motors cost about $15 each when you bought them new.

The inventor's knowledge of business and cost analysis was minimal. He never bothered to find out what the true cost of the production components would be when he quit using the surplus parts. The project was a manufacturing disaster because the licensee had to pay for a complete redesign and a massive search for parts and pieces that would fit the design-to-cost parameters required to make the device cheap enough to service the market.

This might not be something you want to hear, but you must spend part of your time researching the cost and availability of the components that you're designing with and what the cost and availability will be to reproduce these parts and pieces if and when the product is commercialized. If you don't, you might be designing a product that is technically feasible but economically unrealistic.

Availability during the production phase is another concern. I can't recall the number of projects I've had in my career that were delayed or threatened with cancellation because we couldn't get the parts and pieces we need in the quantities or on the delivery schedules needed to make the market timeframes.

When I was working on Teddy Ruxpin for Worlds of Wonder, we needed a special chip to control the servomotors in the eyes, nose and mouth of the animated character. The designers had chosen a great part made by a major semiconductor manufacturer that was used to control the shutter and iris in cameras. The parts were available and listed in the catalog.

The problem was that the chip's usefulness in the camera industry was dwindling. The manufacturer was selling off their inventory, had no plans to manufacture any more parts, and had planned to discontinue the component in a few months.

We spent countless hours in meetings both in the US and Hong Kong convincing the manufacturer to bring the part back off their discontinued list.

When you decide on parts and pieces for your inventions, do the best research you can to make sure that you haven't designed with parts that are hard to get or are scheduled for obsolesce and discontinuation before you can get to market.

Another problem is the labor cost involved. Inventors rarely keep track of the time it took to build a prototype, nor are they interested in performing a time–study analysis for the various proposed manufacturing methods. It's not what they're good at or interested in.

Consider the availability, pricing, and industry acceptance of the materials and manufacturing standards you set and build into your designs. Part of the final evaluation of your inventions for purchase will hinge on the realistic assessment of the true costs in mass production.

The manufacturer will look closely at this component because it affects the costs, investments, and selling price of the item.

Learning Curve

Will it require public education or usage learning?

The world of marketing has two distinct attitudes—product push and market pull (page 19).

Of the two, market pull is much easier for an inventor to attack because you don't have to educate the potential licensee to the merits and advantages of your invention. Of course, they don't have to educate their public either.

For example, VCRs, which are commonly used today, were introduced during the 1960's. It took over fifteen years to educate the public about the advantages of being able to watch the programming of their choice at the time of their choice.

If your invention is radical and not yet understood by the public, it might require public education before people understand its benefits and are willing to buy it.

Even though your invention is smaller, more economical, and overall a better solution to an existing need than the current products, if the public does not immediately perceive this benefits package, they won't buy.

Having been on the inside of several firms' new product development groups where we were considering the manufacturing of tens of millions of dollars worth of products each year, I can assure you that if you're proposing a new concept the two questions that most manufacturers will ask about any new idea or invention are:

- Will the end user believe that there are financial advantages to purchasing the product?

- Does it fill an obvious need and are we targeting a consumer defined need that's easy for them to recognize and identify with?

The best example I've encountered in recent years is a wonderful mortgage reduction payment program. A local agent for the program contracted with me to deliver the program for him at public seminars.

The concept is simple and effective in that it will lower your mortgage substantially over a 5 to 10 year period by having you make bi-weekly payments rather than monthly payments. The annual result is that you make thirteen payments instead of twelve. The savings in interest are substantial and once you've gotten used to making two payments a month (for ½ your regular monthly payment) it becomes a matter of habit.

Unfortunately, the project never got off the ground. I was paid to prepare the presentations but the local agent never got anybody to attend the seminars. The reason was that the public does not understand either the process or the benefits and as a result the program failed miserably.

Making Life Easier

Does it make, or appear to make, life easier for the user and does the user immediately think that this invention will make their tasks or responsibilities less cumbersome to handle?

When you go to the doctor, you are asked, "what's wrong or where does it hurt?"

Manufacturers who are seriously looking at your invention will look at where their market is hurting and whether or not you invention solves that problem. Most people don't engage in preventative measures for anything so the best products for rapid market acceptance are those that address a specific concern that the consumer has voiced and is willing to pay for an answer to.

Firms that are serious about licensing your inventions will consider the cost of educating the public to the merits of your invention and add those costs into their decisions about going to market with it.

The need for training on a new product or concept isn't necessarily bad news. Rapid change in products creates a potential requirement for the users to be trained in their proper and effective usage. For example, computer software has spawned an entire industry to provide third-party books and training for the products.

Sometimes, the manufacturer can include the training as a part of the overall product package and these costs should also be factored into the final price of the item.

For example, there is a software company called Lacerte. They make some of the best commercial tax preparation software in the world. Their software package is sold on an annual license basis because the tax laws change each year.

Because the preparation of tax returns is critical, Lacerte wants to make sure that anyone using their software knows exactly how it works and how to use it to their client's best results. They mandate that training accompany the revisions that occur each year. When you complete the paid training session, you are given a certificate of completion and the update to the software.

In this example the training requirement is a valuable asset because it guarantees that the people who use the product will pay for the training to use it properly and reduce liabilities and risk of error.

When designing your products, look closely at the need for instruction manuals, installation manuals, operation and training manuals, and public education or training. If there is either an actual requirement or a potential need for training, consider it a design element and develop the training as a part of the package.

Although you may not want to, or be in a position to create the education and training component yourself, the potential licensee might think that you've overlooked it if you don't address the issue, and this could cause them to question the overall research that went into the design of the product itself.

Durability Factor

Will it have durability?

Before you run back to workshop and redesign your product with bulletproof parts, consider that this question has two parts:

- What is considered to be the desired durability of the product?

- Does your invention match these requirements?

Not too many years ago, many products were purchased, repaired, maintained, and passed on for generations as a part of the life of the product. With the rapid obsolescence of products due to technological improvements and reduced cost (more bang for the buck), long–term durability might not be as desirable as it once was.

Some things are more marketable if they last longer, but only if the public is willing to pay for this durability. Often times, however, the public would prefer less durability with an accompanying lower cost.

Look at the hand-held calculator market as a prime example. When they were first released in the 1970's, they cost a fortune and were touted as the answer to everyone's arithmetic needs.

They were designed to solve the most sophisticated engineering math problems and were packaged in what could only be described as upscale designs. The price and performance were ridiculous based on today's standards but professionals spent millions of dollars to acquire what they thought would be the answer to their mathematical inabilities.

The calculator industry realized that the real money was in mass merchandising a cheap calculator that everyone could afford. So they decided to create low-cost, reduced performance units that everyone could afford and if it broke, they could toss it out and buy another one.

The result is that today for $1 you can buy a calculator that would have cost $50 back then. Granted it's not as rugged, you can't repair it, and probably can't even change the batteries, but it works for about a year or so.

Digital watches are another area where the low-cost, low-reliability factor helped spur mass marketing.

Prior to the digital watch revolution, most watches were kept for a long time. (Remember watch repair shops? Seen any lately?) Watches were expensive and many were in gold cases because they were a treasured possession to be passed down from generation to generation.

Several firms offered inexpensive watches but weren't widely accepted because they were mechanical, subject to breakdown, and cost a lot to maintain. The basic premise was OK but people resented spending a lot of money to repair a cheap watch.

Timex introduced inexpensive wristwatches for the masses that were reliable and rugged. Takes a lickin' and keeps on tickin'! That's been the Timex motto for over 35 years and has made Timex the most popular and recognized watch brand in North American history.

When digital watches arrived on the scene, I bought one of the original stainless steel LED digital watches back in 1973. It cost $175 and had two functions—it either worked or it didn't. It was designed to last forever but because it had limited functions, it was rapidly overshadowed by newer versions that had more bells and whistles.

The watch industry realized that most people didn't care if a digital watch was an heirloom—people just wanted a nifty new accurate way to tell time. The current result is a $1 watch that tells time better than $10,000 gold case mechanical ones.

Of course they don't last very long but who cares as long as they tell time accurately for their intended lifetime?

Which are you targeting, and have you created and designed your product to match these criteria? If you're targeting one set of criteria and have designed for the other, the manufacturer might not accept your invention because you didn't meet your own standards.

Start-Up Costs

Are the start-up and tooling investments realistic and can it be manufactured with existing tools and equipment?

Consider that 10-cent plastic items may cost thousands in tooling to produce. Thousands of wonderful inventions are rejected each year because they are not economical to produce. They work great, but the public won't pay the price needed to recover the tooling costs.

The public cares little or nothing about the actual cost to produce something. All they're concerned about is the relative cost and value to them.

Manufacturers who are embarking on new products and projects look carefully at the total number of units that have to be made and sold to recover the tooling investment. They also look to see if they can use or modify existing tooling and equipment so they don't have to invest in completely new tooling.

One of the advantages of approaching manufacturers in an industry where they are producing related goods is that there is a good possibility for tooling to exist that might be used at a reduced cost.

I had a client that had invented a new payroll calculator that had plug-in cartridges that contained the latest in tax laws and deductions. I went to Hong Kong and found that if we tooled the case and other components from scratch that we'd be looking at well over $60,000 before we saw a single part.

I located a firm that had been manufacturing desktop calculators for years. They had several designs that had been discontinued and the tooling was lying on the floor gathering rust.

We found one of the designs that could be modified and used it as the foundation for the payroll calculator. Because we could use existing tooling and have it modified for our use, we saved $50,000 over a new tooling price.

If you have knowledge of, or access to information regarding existing tooling or tooling that can be modified for use with your invention be sure to include the information in your promotional materials for licensing. It could become a critical factor in the licensing of your idea.

Competition

What, if any, is the existing competition, does the competition have good acceptance, and is there room for a new product?

One of the things that inventors fear is seeing something similar to their ideas already because they immediately assume that their innovation won't be accepted.

Although it's great to be first, sometimes it's safer to let somebody else pioneer the marketplace and make all the expensive mistakes for you. Actually, having a competitive item or items already accepted by the marketplace proves that there is a lucrative marketplace for the idea—not that there is no room for improvements or competition.

When I took the job of Director of Engineering for Entex in 1980, Mattel had pioneered the electronic handheld game market and already proven that it could be lucrative.

Mattel started the trend in 1976 with the Road Race and baseball games and sold over 500,000 of each for three years. In 1979, the other toy manufacturers were sufficiently convinced of the merits of electronic games and joined in on the coat tails of Mattel. If the truth were told, every other toy manufacturer in the world who was manufacturing and selling electronic handheld games and toys profited from Mattel's pioneering efforts.

During your development phase, learn as much as you can about prior inventions that are similar to yours and see what kind of market acceptance they have.

Sometimes, looking at what is currently being offered and creating improvements to the item will result in rapid acceptance because the industry is already familiar with the product and its shortcomings.

When you look at existing competition, consider that manufacturers may view competition for an invention in one of two ways:

- They may look at it negatively because the competition is already firmly entrenched.

- They may consider it risk reducing because an established entity has already educated the public about the invention.

Japanese manufacturers are keen students of this philosophy, and they're successful at it too. They didn't invent the calculator, digital watch, or home video game. They followed the American products to the marketplace and looked for ways to improve both the price and performance. Now Japanese products dominate the market even though they were not the first.

As previously noted, teaching people about the relative benefits of your innovation might take too long or be too costly for many manufacturers to consider.

Distribution

Can the distribution channels that are needed to be successful be arranged?

Ultimately, the manufacturer that licenses the rights to your invention will have to take it to market. The basic premise of the channel power chain is to license your invention to a manufacturer that already has, or can arrange for marketing and distribution better than you can. Many items require custom manufacturing plants, new tools, special handling and shipping procedures, and require a sales force or sales outlet to deliver the item to the consumer.

A question these firms will have to ask themselves internally is whether or not the invention can be distributed through existing channels of sales and marketing. A manufacturer who already has a sales and distribution system in place will be more likely to take on your invention than one who has to create sales and distribution from scratch.

For example, when I worked in the security industry as Director of Engineering for Notifier Corporation, we would always look at the existing burglar alarm and security system dealers for the distribution of our latest products and systems.

These were alarm companies that were already heavily marketing and promoting products and services to the communities that they served and adding another of our products to their distribution catalogs was a no-brainer for them.

Chapter 8 contains information on locating potential licensees that are already in related or similar businesses and have an established distribution network.

Because the cost of developing and managing a distribution network is so costly, making sure that there is already a distribution network in place will greatly enhance you chances of licensing your innovation.

Test Run

Can you produce a cheap run to test the product?

Everybody performs some form of test marketing regardless of the answer to this question. For many products, the initial mass merchandising rollout of the product is the test. If it fails, the remaining inventory heads for the shelves at closeout stores at a rapid rate.

Anybody who's ever been involved in production releases of a product recognizes that no matter how much we try, the first version of a product usually has bugs in it or at the very least, hasn't been packaged properly for maximum exposure and acceptance.

Realistically, however, it's in our best interest if we can do a test run cheaply before we commit to large volumes of a product that still has bugs in it or the public wants modified before they'll pay the asking price.

In the worst case, we have a product that fails, causes damage, or loses money, any or all of which spell disaster for the product and potentially for the company.

Logic then dictates that it's always in the best interest of the manufacturer to produce a limited run to test the product from multiple standpoints, including function, durability, manufacturing ease, cost affectivity, test compliance, packaging, consumer acceptance, etc.

However some industries and products do not lend themselves to this wish, no matter how important it might be. For example, injection molded plastic tooling is expensive. Even though you, and the manufacturer, would love to be able to make a few low–volume runs to test the product, it isn't going to happen.

Sometimes, a small run of hand-built prototypes can be assembled for initial market reaction. Teddy Ruxpin was a great example of this. The end product required a fortune in tooling and Don Kingsborough realized that he needed samples to demonstrate to the toy buyers to get them to commit to the product.

One of my initial tasks when I moved to Hong King was to round up enough parts for the inventors to build sixty hand-built prototypes for Don to use as marketing samples.

We had a tough time getting the parts but were successful. The results were phenomenal and Don obtained orders for over 600,000 units based on the performance of the prototypes that he left with the toy buyers to play with and show to their family and friends.

Once the commitment has been made, large dollar amounts will be spent, regardless of whether the product is successful or not.

If your invention cannot be test marketed cheaply or on a reduced scale from the eventual production quantities, you'll be scrutinized far more extensively than an inventor with a product that can be, or has been, test marketed. The commitment to the product is going to cost the manufacturer money to back up the decision to accept your invention.

Protection

Somewhere in the process of considering your invention, the manufacturer is going to want to know what kind and level of proprietary protection is already in place for the product and what protection can be made available if required.

Although this is still a consideration in the overall process of licensing inventions, it no longer carries the weight and importance that it once did with respect to patents. The fast turn–around from inception to market, along with the short life cycle of many products, has caused manufacturers to look at the immediate market acceptance rather than patents.

For example, toys and games have a typical life cycle of one-year. Since utility patents take from two to five years on average, the market for the toy may come and go before propriety protection can be put in place. In this industry, little is ever patented but much is marketed.

Keep in mind that although a patent may provide you with a selling edge to certain potential licensees, you do not need a patent to market your invention. If you violate other's patents, you've made yourself a target for a lawsuit or rejection by the manufacturer.

The proprietary rights to your invention may or may not be a consideration in its sale. However, prime consideration should be given to the possible violation of other's rights. Be conscientious during your design phase and conduct novelty searches on all products that might be covered under pre-existing patents and be careful to not violate existing trademarks and copyrights.

Final thoughts and considerations

As previously stated, these questions are not designed to make you wrong or to dissuade you from either your inventing or marketing efforts.

They are, however, offered here, as a form of safety net to help ensure your success by eliminating the reasons potential licensees needs to say no thank you and ignore your efforts.

The Channel Power Chain

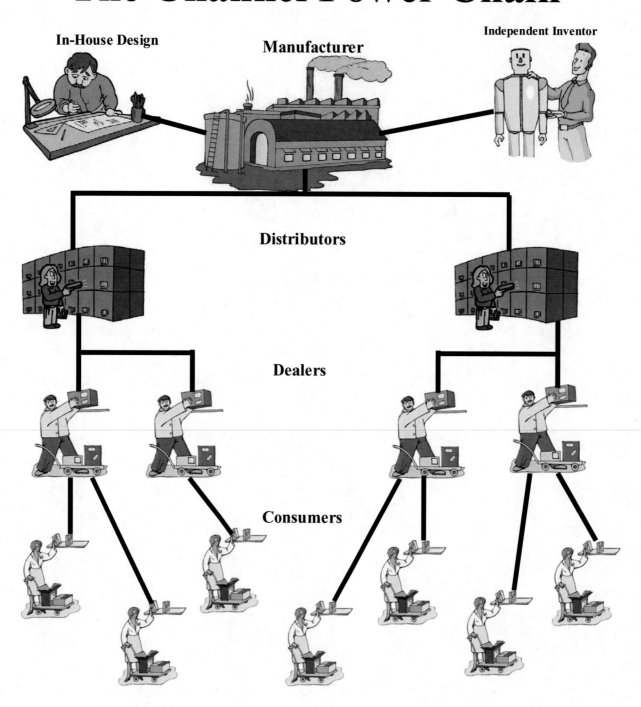

Chapter 8
How To Make A Solicitation

Now that you have your product design figured out, your prototype completed, and are ready to find a licensee, it's time for you to make your solicitation and market research mailing to potential licensees.

This is actually a simple, step–by–step process, which incorporates the processes of your solicitation and market research of a potential licensee for your invention in one consolidated effort.

Our experience is that the process works 100 percent of the time. The results may be disappointing if you find that no one wants your invention but the process is guaranteed to produce accurate results if you follow it properly.

And simple isn't necessarily easy. If it were, everybody would be successful. This part of the process can be, and often is, as time consuming, frustrating, and aggravating as anything else in the invention process.

Don't forget to complete your prototype and establish your legal rights, whatever you decide they should be, before you go any further.

Step 1: Getting a List

First you need to locate the existing firms that currently manufacture and market products that are similar to yours, related to yours, or exist in the target marketplace that purchase your type of invention.

The most effective method for doing this is to obtain an industry specific directory for your target market and extract the list from there.

To locate the directories, start at the public library. Go to the reference desk and request Directories in Print by Gale Research Inc. This is the most comprehensive source available. It describes approximately 20,000 active rosters, guides and other print and non-print address lists published in the US and worldwide. Hundreds of additional directories (defunct, suspended and directories that cannot be located) are cited, with status notes, in the title/keyword index.

Directories in Print lists product and service under three different headings:

1. Specific industries and lines of business.

2. Title and key word index.

3. Subject index.

Once you've found the correct subject, title, and product, look up the directory or directories for the industry related to your invention. The lists contain the name, address, phone number, directory price, and a description of what's in the directory.

The information below is a typical listing in the directory. For our example, we've chosen to solicit a board game. Since games are a part of the toy industry, we'll need to get a directory of the toy industry and then break the industry down by categories.

Having looked up the subject of toys we find several directories available. The one we've selected is shown below:

Playthings—Buyers Guide
Geyer-McAllister Publications, Inc.
575 Lexington Ave., 4th Fl
New York, NY 10022-6102 USA
Phone: (212) 689-4411
Fax: (212) 683-7929
Key Personnel: Frank Reysen, Jr., Editor
Former Title: Formerly: Playthings—Directory Issue (1988); Supersedes: Playthings—Who's Who in Importing Issue; Formerly: Playthings—Who Makes It Issue

Description: Publication includes: Lists of toy manufacturers and their suppliers, designers and inventors, manufacturers' representatives, licensor, importers.

Arrangement: Separate alphabetical sections for manufacturers and their suppliers; manufacturers' representatives are geographical. Indexes: Manufacturer product, supplier product, trade name. Entries include: Company name, address, phone, description of products manufactured or lines carried. Also Includes: Calendar of trade fairs.

Frequency: Annual; December.
Subject Descriptor(s): Toy industry
Subject Category: Retail, Wholesale, and Consumer Service Industries

How to purchase a copy of the Playthings Buyers Guide:
The Buyers Guide is available with a paid subscription to Playthings for an Internet special rate of $29 for the US, Canada and Mexico and $69 for all other countries. The Buyers Guide is also available individually for $50.

To order the Buyers Guide separately, send a check for $50 made out to *Playthings* to Playthings Magazine, Post Office Box 2754, High Point, N.C. 27215. For credit card orders for a Playthings subscription or the Buyers Guide, call 1-800-309-3332.

Listings from the **Playthings** directory. The listings on the left are by category and the listings on the right show the contact information.

GAMES—Card	Binney & Smith Inc Crayola Products Art Materials Div 1100 Church La PO Box 431 Easton PA 18042 215-253-6271.

GAMES—Card

Adams S S Company
Amuse Inc
Ardsley Dist Co
Aristoplay Limited
Arlane Mfg Co
Avalon Hill Game Co
Baron/Barclay Bridge Suppliers
Baron/Scott Enterprises
Bermiss-Jason Corp
Bradley Co Milton
Brechner Dan & Co Inc
Cadaco
Collated Products Corp
Cambor Enterprises Inc
Creative Toys Inc
D-A-S-H Incorporated
Davis-Grabowski Inc
Dollsandreams Inc

Binney & Smith Inc Crayola Products Art Materials Div 1100 Church La PO Box 431 Easton PA 18042 215-253-6271.
Bizzy Bee Willow Av York Beach ME 03910.
Black Hawk Hobby Dist 14225 Hansberry Rd Rockton IL 61072 815-624-7277.
Blake & Conroy PO Box 189 Peconic NY 11958 516-734-6894.
Bland & Glennon Inc 200 5 Av Rm 326 New York NY 10010 212-675-3790. Fax: 212-463-0811.
Blarney Co PO Box 127 Bel Air MD 21014 301-879-7967.
Bleyer Industries Inc 229 Broadway Lynbrook NY 11563 516-887-1100.
Bliss House 9 Hampden St Springfield MA 01103 413-737-0757. Fax 413-781-3770.
Blocks & Marbles Brand Toys PO Box 807 Crawfordsville IN 47933 800-446-7843.
Blue Box 1107 Broadway Suite 905 New York NY 212-242-1313.
Blythe Imports 5006 Robles Dr Upper Marlboro MD 20772 301-627-5281.
Boise Cascade Specialty Paperboard Div Latex Fiber Products Beaver Falls NY 13305 315-346-1111.
Bolder Creations PO Box 17785 Boulder CO 80308 303-665-5445.
Bolink R/C Cars Inc 420 Hosea Rd Lawrenceville GA 30245 404-963-0252 Fax: 404-963-7334.

Step 2: Using the Directory

Order the appropriate directory. When the directory arrives, find all the firms who appear to be involved in the manufacturing and marketing of products or services that are similar to, and/or related to your invention.

Enter the information for these firms into a database. Don't prejudge or pre-qualify any of these firms. The more possibilities you examine, the greater the chance of your invention being reviewed by the manufacturer(s) that is looking for items like what you're offering.

Here's an example of refining the list. Since we're developing and soliciting a new board game, we need to refine the list of approximately 2,000 generic toy and game firms into ones that that currently manufacture and/or distribute games and puzzles. It's not that the firms who offer action figures and baby carriages are not good companies, it's that they don't specialize in our particular type of toy.

Once we've refined the search to the game and puzzle manufacturers, we can now cross reference their information to pick out their contact information including name, address, phone, fax, e-mail, and web site.

Step 2½: Telephoning

Weird huh? A Step 2½? It's given a ½ because each time I'm asked this question, I flinch because there is no correct answer to it. Here's the question: "What do I do first—call the companies or write them first?"

The reason I have a problem with the question is that I don't know. In my own business dealings, I actually do some of my solicitation and market research by writing first and others I do by calling first.

If I have to voice a preference, I'd go with writing first and then following up by phone. However, if you prefer to call them first, here's the procedure:

- Call each of the firms asking if they accept outside submissions.

- If they say no, put the names aside. There are times of the year (before a tradeshow, after a tradeshow or during litigation) that manufacturers might not be open to outside inventors (if at all). Contact this list again in about six months.

- If they say yes, ask the name (and correct spelling) of the person handling outside submissions and if the firm requires any forms to be signed prior to reviewing the submission.

Step 3: Cover Letter

The cover letter has 8 important elements as follows for some very specific reasons. See sample letter on page 112.

1. Letterhead. At this time, it doesn't matter whether you are an individual or a business.

2. Date. Always date your letter including the year.

3. Attention: Director of New Product Development. This salutation is a job function rather than a job title (vice president of engineering, vice president of development, etc.). If you don't know specifically who to solicit, by addressing the job function, the letter will get to the correct final destination.

4. Dear New Product Director. This doesn't sound too wonderful but it is politically correct (at least at this time anyway).

5. "Enclosed you will find ..." is a generic opening that doesn't give away any proprietary information.

6. "If you have ..." lets the manufacturer know that you are interested in licensing the product so they don't have to read your mind. This is an unsolicited submission. Don't ask them to incur additional expense by sending it back to you. Besides, once an idea is planted the seed begins to grow. Maybe no today and yes tomorrow.

7. Disclaimer. The disclaimer allows the manufacturer to review the product openly and without fear of legal problems. If they get serious and want to take a further look, they'll probably send you a nondisclosure or disclaimer of their own to keep their own in-house attorneys happy. They might have seen your invention, or a variation on it before. They're not going to take a chance on being sued by you for stealing your invention when they may have seen it previously or developed it a while ago. Don't be afraid of these documents! These companies are less interested in a lawsuit than you are and if you don't sign and submit this form, you're dead from the start!

8. "Regardless of your decision" is a way of soliciting their feedback about your invention.

Step 4: Solicitation and Market Research Package

This consists of three primary elements:

Step 4.1: Caution

The caution is used as a wrapper around the description and photos. It helps to ensure that the wrong person doesn't open the confidential part of the package. See sample caution below.

Step 4.2: Description

A description (two pages maximum) of the product will be inside the caution wrapper. This particular copy should be written in what's commonly called marketing puff style. You've seen it used extensively in advertising and after all, you're advertising, aren't you? Remember that facts tell, but stories sell.

You'll want to arouse the interest of the manufacturers but not bore them with details that they don't need.

Because you understand what the product is all about doesn't necessarily mean that you've conveyed that same levels of understanding in your write up. You might want to get somebody to read, review, critique and see if they understand your description after you write it.

You're trying to convince the manufacturer that you have the greatest idea since the invention of sliced bread, and you've only have a few lines on a piece of paper to convince them. Do not use the patent claims (if you're patented already)!

Sample Cover Letter

John Doe[1]

123 Any Place Street
Any Where, US 98765-4321
[999] 555-1212

Current Date and Year[2]

Acme Widgets Company[3]

Attention: Director of New Product Development

9876 Last Street

Someplace NY 98765

Dear New Product Director[4]

[5] Enclosed you will find a photograph and a description of an exciting new product for the upcoming season. The item is fully explained inside the information package.

[6] If you have an interest in obtaining the exclusive rights to this product, I may be reached at the above phone number. If you find that the item does not fit into your current plans, please feel free to retain the enclosed information for your files.

[7] My invention relating to toy industry is submitted to you on a non-confidential basis and its submission does not obligate you in any way. I understand that upon submission of my idea, you will promptly review and consider whether you desire to offer me a royalty agreement to use the idea. In the event that I do not enter an agreement with you, I understand that you assume no obligation and that any claim(s) that I may have shall be based upon patents, trademarks, copyrights, or other rights I might now have or will obtain on my idea.

[8] Regardless of your decision, I would appreciate your comments, as these will assist me in determining your interests. Thank you for your time. I sincerely hope that you find the product as interesting, exciting and profitable as I do.

Very truly yours

John Doe

John Doe

Enclosures:

Sample Caution

This package of information contains a new product submission and has been sealed to protect the proprietary interests of both your firm and me. The disclaimer is my acknowledgment of both of our rights in submitting my ideas to you.

If you require that I sign your firm's nondisclosure form before you review the enclosed product submissions, please return the unopened documents, along with your forms, and I'll sign and resubmit the entire package immediately.

Since I don't have the name of the person in your firm who is currently responsible for reviewing new product submissions, I would appreciate your passing the package along to the correct person.

Thank you.

A single sheet description will be adequate to get the firm's attention. Sometimes you'll need two pages of material. NEVER send more than two pages—they are not interested nor do they have the time to read more material than can be contained in two pages.

The sample description shown below is for Chuck Monary's Road Toad. We created it with Microsoft Publisher as a two-sided tri-fold brochure. We're grateful to Chuck for his permission to reproduce it here.

The Road Toad appeared on the covers of FAO Schwarz and Hammacher Schlemmer Christmas catalogs as well as included in Nieman Marcus, Sky Mall, J. C. Penny and more catalogs. It has already been on ABC TV twice and CNN in Philadelphia. It has also caught the interest of Skecher shoes, Pepsi, and Coke to use in their TV commercials in promoting their products.

The *Road-Toad*™ — is a pedal-powered, single speed three-wheeled vehicle that can be used on any hard surface.

The hottest new idea of the year, described as *"A vehicle that's too much fun."*

The *Road-Toad*™ has been in development for over a year, and has been thoroughly field tested.

Its designers have incorporated safety, ease of transportation, high efficiency, and lots of fun in a pedal powered vehicle that's suitable for adults and kids.

Whazup With Performance?

The *Road-Toad*™:

- *F*eatures recumbent pedal power to provide maximum power for forward, reverse, and coasting.

- *I*s more maneuverable, faster, and can take greater impacts than the bumper cars of yester-year.

- *C*an also be used as a futuristic transport vehicle.

- *F*eatures reflexive 360° maneuvering, controlled with ram-thrust, side mounted, steering handles.

- *U*ses control mechanisms that include a reverse clutch and hand brake integrated into the ram-thrust controls.

- *I*ncorporates a body made of space age molded plastic that provides strength and flexibility to distribute the force of impact without jolting the rider.

 What about proprietary protection?

All preliminary work for establishing proprietary rights has been done.

The *Road-Toad*™and all of its related companion products are fully registered, have passed preliminary patent examinations and have been deemed as patent pending..

All related packaging copy and literature is copyrighted.

Based on the preliminary filings and diligence, counsel has advised us that full patent registration and protection may be expected following the completion of all formal filing and review procedures by the United States Patent and Trademark office.

Step 4.3: Photographs

A picture is definitely worth a thousand words when it comes to submitting new ideas for serious consideration. I'm going to take a departure from my past recommendations and say that you've got two choices on the photos:

Choice #1 is to take 35mm color pictures with a camera. Reprints are cheap (approximately 25 cents each) and the detail on the prints is very clear.

If you would like to, you can take digital pictures. However, after you print out the print, can you clearly see all the details of your prototype? If anything is fuzzy or unclear, use a 35mm camera.

Two shots are plenty because any more than that will confuse people. If your invention is something that creates a change, like a cleaning solution, take a tip from the advertising agencies and show the before and after shots.

If it's appropriate, put some props in the picture with the invention. As an example, if you're making an accessory item for fashion dolls, put the dolls in the picture. Don't over-do the props—keep it simple.

If you've made a sample of the packaging, include it in the photos. It not only shows the manufacturer that you've taken the concept on to this point, but it also gives them some additional information for consideration that they don't have to look up themselves.

Put a label on the back of the photographs. Include the product name, your name (or company name, be consistent with the letter), address, city, state and ZIP code, telephone number and the month and year. If they are going to keep only one thing, it will probably be the photograph. WEB SITE

Choice #2 is to do what we did with the Road Toad and that's to use either artist's drawings or digital photographs and incorporate them right into the advertising brochure itself. If you decide to incorporate them into the brochure, that you MUST use high quality paper and set the printer for a photographic quality of resolution to ensure their clarity and overall impact.

Step 5: Mailing

After you've prepared the materials for the solicitation and market research package, sign each letter, fold them, and insert them in the #10 (legal) size envelopes. Below your return address, put the words: Return Service Requested (so that you get their new address and can resend the package).

Now that you are ready to mail the envelopes, here are some guidelines to follow:

- Don't mail any more letters than you can follow up on in a week (for example, mail 25 letters, follow up on 25; then mail another 25 and follow up on them the next week).

- Do not wait longer than 10 days from the date of mailing to do the telephone follow up. If you can't make the follow up calls in that time frame, don't mail the packages or you'll be wasting your time.

After you drop the packages in the mail, you may start to see some of the letters returned to you. This is normal since all business have a mortality factor and end up going out of business after they have been listed in the directories.

You may also get a letter that says "We're not interested now, but contact me later." It is advisable to call them as soon as possible, regardless of what the letter says. These people have expressed a positive interest in your products and they should be pursued (politely but firmly) until they either say yes or no.

Don't be obnoxious, but call and thank them personally and remind them that you'll be following up with them again in a matter of weeks or months, whatever is appropriate at the time.

Regardless of the outcome, these people are a valuable source of feedback either now or in the future because they responded immediately which puts them in the category of rational business people and you can probably get some solid feedback if you elect to contact them for their reasons for rejection.

(NOTE: The two exceptions are if they don't handle anything like your product or are currently not accepting outside submissions!)

You'll probably see some form letters that say thanks but no thanks, so don't be surprised.

Included somewhere in the returns will be letters from companies taking you up on your offer to sign their disclaimer agreement before they'll look at the package. Do as they ask and return the package ASAP.

It no longer matters because you've now *gone public* with your ideas and are using the public recognition of your *date of discovery* to assist you in proving any *rights of ownership* claims or disputes that may occur in the future.

Step 6: Telephone Follow Up

When you call the firms that you have sent your solicitation and market research package to, it's critical that you keep accurate records so that you can track your progress. The sample form below has proven to be the most efficient format whether you handwrite the information or reenter it into a computer.

Be sure to take notes regarding what the people have to say. This feedback is coming from the people who know the current state of the industry and you may need it to make modifications to the product to make it acceptable.

If you are uncomfortable with performing the follow up procedures yourself or if time will not permit it, I strongly recommend hiring somebody else to perform the work for you.

Students who are theater arts, drama, or sales and marketing majors usually like to talk to people and aren't bothered when they receive a rejection.

These individuals should be schooled in the basics of the product and turned loose to perform the follow up work for you.

Note that we have selected the name, "Terry", so that either a male or female can perform the initial follow up work.

Using the guidelines outlined below, and in conjunction with the written follow up sheets instruct the individual to probe for data and information regarding what needs to be done to sell them on the concept.

Regardless of whether you do it yourself or hire someone to make the calls for you, when contacting the firms, politely ask the person who answers the phone who you should be talking to regarding a new product solicitation that you made.

Under no circumstances should you divulge to the person who answers the phone the nature of your new product solicitation until such time as they identify themselves as being the person to talk to.

Many companies have very strict rules regarding the divulging of new product information to the wrong people. In some cases, companies believe that it compromises their legal integrity and will cause your solicitation and market research to be rejected because of it.

Sample Telephone Follow Up Form

Company: Phone:

Date:

Hi, This is Terry from _____'s Office.

We recently sent your firm an unsolicited product offering directed to the Director of New Product Development. Who would that person be or who would have been most likely to have received the information?

Do you remember seeing it or reviewing it? Yes _____ No _____ Resend _____

From what you've seen and read, what do you like or dislike about the product?

Are you interested in seeing more material on the product? Yes ____ No ____

Can you recommend another firm or individual? Yes ___ No ____

NOTES:

You will find that manufacturers fall into categories:

1. Firms that are listed erroneously as a company that would be interested in your inventions. Cross them off your list and go to the next manufacturer.

2. Firms that are not a manufacturer but are listed as such in the directories. Cross them off your list and go to the next manufacturer.

3. Firms that do not accept outside inventions. Put them on a list to follow up on in approximately six months.

   A recent phenomenon spurred on by the filing of nuisance lawsuits against companies by inventors who believe that they have been ripped-off are, are firms who do not accept outside solicitations. Regardless of whether you believe the inventors have been wronged or whether you think that it's unfair that somebody else's action affect whether or not your product is reviewed is academic. This industry makes up its own rules and since it's their game, they get to decide who plays.

4. Firms that sometimes do and sometimes don't accept outside inventions. If this is not the time when they are accepting outside inventions, ask when they are. If their answer is vague, put them on a list to follow up on in approximately six months.

5. Firms that accept outside inventions, but only through an agent of their choice. Find out who their agent is and how to contact them. Then contact the agent.

   A broker or agent will act as a middleman between you and their company. Hasbro is famous for this approach so be prepared for it.

   The logic behind the move is that the agent acts as a buffer between inventors and the companies themselves, thereby insulating these manufacturers from direct contact with the product and potential lawsuits.

   The idea sounds good at first review, but in reality, it's another way of saying, "we're not interested." The agents will typically charge you between $300 and $600 just to look at your product and will give you NO GUARANTEES regarding either their showing it to the manufacturers or if they do show it, what the manufacturer's acceptance will be.

   This might be OK, but the agent's usually only represent between 6 to 15 manufacturers. If you want your product shown to 50 firms, you'll have to contract with 5 separate agents at an average of $500 each, or an additional $2,500 just to have these agents review your product.

   The expediency of using these agents is questionable at best, so consider the costs and relative merits before you decide to pay somebody to look at your idea.

6. Firms that accept outside inventions and are willing to review yours.

    Of course, anybody who expresses a positive interest right now should be contacted immediately without any delays or hesitation. Over 95 percent of all buying is done out of emotion and it's best to strike while the interest is present.

After the initial contacts have been made, and the interested firms have been weeded out, you can contact them yourself for in-depth discussions as to what they want and how they would like to proceed.

If you only have one prototype, which is pretty much standard for most new inventions, you can't afford to ship it around the country and have it lost or broken.

With the advent of low cost, easy to use camcorders and video editing software, it's easy to make a two-three minute demonstration video that will let you clone your product. If you don't want to do it yourself, students majoring in videography will be thrilled to make an *infomercial* of your invention for a low price just to get the experience.

The advantages are:

•   You can have as many "copies" made as you need for a few dollars.

•   You get an accurate representation of your invention.

•   You get to demonstrate it in the manner that you envisioned it.

•   You don't risk the loss of your one and only prototype.

When you have explained your invention to someone and they appear to be interested in opening negotiations for the rights to the product, get their complete information and then begin the process of licensing negotiations.

I have been on both sides of the licensing fence and I can tell you from experience that there is an unwritten, but commonly accepted, process for performing this task, which is covered in the next chapter.

Chapter 9
Royalty and Licensing Agreement

Congratulations! You've done your homework, performed the solicitation and market research, and a firm has responded positively. Don't order a new Lamborghini yet! You've still got the licensing agreement ahead of you and based on years of experience, this is the legal and financial minefield that costs inventors the most time, money, grief, and aggravation.

> "Of the more than 1 million patents in force today, only five percent are ever licensed or earn royalties. In fact, some 500,000 of them will expire halfway through their 20-year life spans, because the inventors or companies that registered them stopped paying the maintenance fees."
>
> *Bright Ideas Patented, Rarely Used*
> *Wired magazine April 2002*

Win-win situations are possible but if, and only if, you educate yourself and are prepared to negotiate for what you believe is in your best interests.

Because negotiations are inherently confrontational by their nature, many inventors tend to avoid the particulars or trust the outcome to somebody else. The end result tends to be disastrous because the inventor didn't get involved at a deep enough level to guarantee that the deal was structured to his or her best advantage.

The two ways that a firm will usually acquire the rights to your product are to:

1. Buy the product outright.

2. Buy it for royalties based on a percentage of the selling price.

Unless you have something special going that gives you either a super strong or a super weak position at the bargaining table, it is doubtful that you'll be selling your concept outright. It's usually too risky and these days most manufacturers won't crapshoot that heavily.

Of course, if you have a patented or copyrighted process that'll enhance their product line and guarantee that they'll double their business in six months, you might get an outright sales offer but don't count on it. What's more likely to happen is that they'll offer you a royalty agreement for a percentage of the sale price of the item when it's completed.

Show Me The Money

You'll be paid based on the wholesale selling price of the product. Automobile advertising and selling, and the discounted sticker prices, have taught us that the suggested retail-selling price has little validity. It's basically a case of selling the goods or services at whatever price the traffic will bear.

What's probably more important and appropriate is that you're dealing with the manufacturer who's at the top of the distribution chain, and the manufacturer doesn't have any control over the retail-selling price. It's against the fair trade laws for them to do so.

The basic royalties are computed against the wholesale selling price, but these too have some additional elements that enter into the final payments.

Royalties range from around 1 percent to 10 percent of the wholesale selling price and average about 3 percent to 5 percent, depending on the product, category, and price.

You can assume that you will be paid 60 to 90 days after the first shipments and then every quarter. If you're lucky, you might even get monthly royalty checks, but don't count on it.

Here's an example that I've actually used for a board game that we licensed when I was in the toy business. It's a pretty common example and it might just fit exactly into your invention's licensing profile.

Consumer products and some industrial products are calculated on the basis of manufacturing and selling 100,000 units per year. This isn't a magic number but accountants and other business people like to use it as a foundation because it's realistic with respect to the 240 million people in the US and high enough to make the product economically viable and profitable.

Suppose that we have a product that has a suggested retail price of $19.95. The manufacturer publishes a price list to the dealer/distributors offering the product at a wholesale selling price of $10.

Let's also assume that you've negotiated a 5 percent royalty.

Based on these parameters, here's the financial example:

Wholesale price	$10.00
5 percent royalty	x .05
Royalty per item sold	$ .50
Number of units sold	x 100,000
Total royalty received per year	$50,000.00

If your royalties are paid quarterly, you would receive a check for $12,500 every 90 days and your exposure and efforts, after the deal was signed, would be virtually zero.

What happens if the manufacturer reduces the wholesale price? Don't feel that you're getting cheated when this sort of arrangement occurs because high volume clients usually qualify for a discounted price. You'll find that these kinds of discounts are usually accompanied by extremely large orders, so the quantities usually rise rapidly and the overall royalties paid are greater.

You are only entitled to be paid a percentage on what the manufacturer actually bills and gets paid for; these are within the guidelines of the industry.

Discounted wholesale price	$5.00
5 percent royalty	x .05
Royalty per item sold	$ .25
Number of units sold	x 200,000
Total royalty received per year	$50,000.00

You'll only receive royalties on the billing and payments. Giveaways, promotional items, sales samples, and the like are not included in these; so don't expect royalties on these either.

If you think this looks kind of small, consider that in the days when I was in the toy business, most of our handheld games sold to the distributors for $28 each. At a 5 percent royalty, that was $1.40 per game and at 100,000 units sold, the inventor made $140,000 per year for doing nothing.

Special Contract Clauses

As you look over the licensing agreement located on page 50, you'll see a lot of legal terminology and what is commonly referred to as boilerplate. These are the standard terms and conditions that define the operating parameters of the agreement and are usually pretty mundane.

What are not mundane, and should not be overlooked, are the following four areas, which actually determine the critical parts of the agreement, and binds the licensee to a performance standard that helps to ensure that you and your inventions are not exploited unfairly.

Activity Clause

You'll be entitled to receive your royalties, as agreed on, for as long as the product remains active, so the first critical clause is the definition of what actually constitutes an active product.

Activity starts when the contract is signed, and this clause may also include time frames for development, advertising, test marketing as well as actual sales. When the product has been production engineered and is being sold, the product is then considered to be active for any year in which it is shown and advertised, and you'll be entitled to royalties for any sales that are a result of that year's sales.

Make sure that you precisely define every stage of development, evaluation, tooling, testing, advertising, marketing, and actual sales. Also, you must define what constitutes activity after the product has actively entered the marketplace. This can be defined as being actively offered for sale at an annual tradeshow, a minimum dollar amount of sales per month, quarter, year, a minimum quantity of the invention sold in a specified time frame, or a combination of these.

Reversion Clause

The right of rescission or reversion rights have to do with and what happens to the rights after the manufacturer no longer actively pursues the marketing of the product.

This clause is your guarantee that the product automatically reverts to you as soon as the licensee does not actively pursue (test, tool, market or advertise) your invention at the specified tradeshow or when mutually agreed upon activity dates or sales volumes have not been met.

This is actually a win-win situation because if they aren't marketing it, why should they keep it? On the other hand, if they aren't pushing it, why should they be allowed to keep the rights to it?

This may not seem like a big thing, but someday you may be the person with the rights to a product that is getting set to enjoy a second round of popularity or have found another source of distribution and you have the rights to the invention to peddle all over again.

If you want any of the tooling or production designs, for whatever reasons, it's up to you to make appropriate arrangements for them because they're not automatically yours, only the rights to the invention (unless, of course, you paid for and supplied the tooling or designs to begin with).

Artistic Review Clause

UNPAID CONSULTANT

A concern of inventors is whether they will have any control over their inventions once the rights have been licensed. The right of artistic review clauses are important if your invention has aesthetic characteristics that you don't want changed or compromised, such as external packaging, character designs, color schemes, trademarks, and other similar items.

Artistic review may include materials specifications, testing criteria, manufacturing guidelines, or other elements that are important to you and where you are the best expert to guide them in their efforts.

Generally, these clauses stipulate that you, as the inventor, will be given, at no charge, a complete set of samples or specifications prior to the item going into production. You will be required to approve each item, in writing, prior to its release to production and marketing.

There is a crucial caveat to be observed here and that is to NOT get overzealous about being the only person who can approve something before the product can be manufactured or marketed.

We worked with a client several years ago that had a device called the Canbuster. He decided that since he had invented the device that he was the world's leading authority on how it should be engineered and manufactured.

As with many licensed prototypes, the Canbuster needed production engineering to make it practical for mass assembly. The inventor insisted on tremendous involvement in the production engineering including meetings, parts specifications, and generally "bugging" the design engineers.

All of this was OK until he submitted a bill to the licensee for his "consulting services." He didn't understand, nor was he willing to accept the fact, that his compensation would come in the form of royalties when the Canbuster was sold and that since he had volunteered his expertise during the development stages, that he was, for all practical purposes, an unpaid consultant.

The inventor refused to back down and insisted that the licensee was obligated to pay him for his time and expenses. The situation escalated out of control and the licensee voluntarily defaulted on the contract and returned the rights, parts, and everything else to the inventor thus ending the project.

Audit Clause

This is a standard clause that usually states that you and/or your authorized representative has the right, on a specified time interval and at times that are mutually convenient to both parties, to review the sales of the item and verify that the royalties paid are true, correct, and complete.

Take someone with you (a CPA) to review the books. It is unlikely that in these times there are two sets of books, but there could be a creative accountant. Your royalties are a part of the gross dollar figures, not the net dollars.

Some examples of recently licensed products:

Splash N' Dash -*Spring 2000/2001 - Licensed to Sport Fun, Inc*

Splash 'n Dash is a unique, modular, outdoor water toy line that allows children to assemble an endless variety of outdoor water-sprayer play layouts. Created by Elizabeth Dowey, the product consists of simple male/female connectors and multi-shaped base and post components that are easily assembled to spray nozzles that spew water in variety of shapes and patterns while driving fun water driven sprayer mechanisms

Star Wars® Electronic X-wing fighter simulator - Independent Inventor Licensed Product

A StarWars®, accessory, toy line, created by Larry Whiley, Peter Douglas and Wayne Swan, consisting of two StarWars® spaceships (X-Wing Fighter & Millennium Falcon) and an innovative, electronic, flight yoke simulating real flying maneuvers. Licensed to Hasbro

Wd-40 "Value Spring Pack promotion" Licensed Product

Promotional program premiums, created, designed and developed by Paul Lapidus, Bill Ulch & TTG/NewFuntiers, consisting of two on-pack tube holders and a free mail-in "Tuff Stuff" scrubber/scraper brush. Licensed to WD-40.

"It's a done deal! Today I signed the license agreement and worked out the distribution of royalties between Kim's company and my company.

Thank you for your help in making this deal work for everyone involved, and a special thanks to you for your continued interest in my products. – Harry Dantolan, Inventor of the Tolanizer exercise device

Most baseball fans hope to walk away from a baseball game with a foul ball trophy. That hope was shared by inventor Stan Boyd, of Santee, Calif., who came a finger-tip (or five) away from snagging a baseball at a San Diego Padres game about 20 years ago. Remembering an idea his father gave him, Boyd created the **Game Hat.** It looks like an ordinary baseball cap, but when held by the visor's handle, the Game Hat catches foul balls. When the ball hits, a pocket in the back pops out and traps the ball. The hat has been tested in batting cages at 70 mph as well as at major league baseball games. In fact, Boyd has caught three foul balls at three different Padres games with his hat.

Family barbecues are fun any summer season. Barbecuing accidents are not. Frank Bartels, of Carmel Valley, Calif., invented the heat-reflective **ProcoverPlus** with the idea of minimizing the number of trips to the emergency room. The **ProcoverPlus** is designed to slip over a propane tank to help keep it safe. Each year, there are about 5,300 instances of fires and explosions associated with improper use, storage or accidental situations connected to propane barbecues and propane tanks. Grease fires are one common and unpredictable event that overheats tanks. When overheated, the tank vents propane, resulting in flash fires and explosions. Made of the same material used to protect space crafts, firefighters and HAZMAT crews from heat, ProcoverPlus covers are currently available in selected Ace Hardware, TrueValue Hardware stores The product sells for $24.95.

Chapter 10
Invention Marketing
Companies

If you watch TV, read magazines, or listen to the radio, sooner or later you're bound to hear an advertisement for an invention marketing company. These firms spend a fortune convincing inventors to let them develop and market their inventions for huge fees with no guarantees for performance or results.

The information in this chapter will give you the truth about the scams, rip-offs, and plain boldfaced lies that many of the firms are engaged in when it comes to taking inventors money and doing nothing of value for it.

Harsh words you say? You bet, and they're well deserved. First, let me categorically say four things:

1. ALL inventors need some help at some time. We've long past the point of being able to do everything ourselves to make our efforts profitable.

2. There's nothing wrong with soliciting and paying for services. We do it every day from paying someone to dry clean our clothes to having our brakes adjusted.

3. If you decide to pay for services, make sure that you get what you pay for. NEVER buy services based on best efforts. Always have a specific list of items that you are going to receive in return for your money.

4. Make sure that what you're paying for is something that you need. Most of the invention marketing scams centers around the concept that they will deliver certain items, and they do, in fact, deliver them. The question becomes: Why would I want these items?

Why Does It Happen?

Inventors are innovators, which puts you ahead of the average individual. Because you're ahead of the thinking process of others, you're somewhat alone in your ideas and tend to become somewhat isolated in your concepts. You're trying to promote something that others have not thought of yet.

This tends to make you vulnerable to those who profess to understand what you're going through and seem to understand your needs and feelings.

It's at this time of vulnerability that you usually become aware of the firms that are offering you their services in return for money. You'd probably never consider doing business with these people under ordinary circumstances, but the uniqueness and isolation of your present situation makes you vulnerable.

If you've examined the process described in this book and agree with the logic, you should be able to make a judgment about anybody who offers to perform services for you for a fee.

I believe that because there are two, and only two, ways to get an outside submission of an invention considered by a company: know someone inside the company or research and solicit them yourself. The logical sequence for approaching that manufacturer and determining if there is a market for your invention should be the guideline for deciding what needs to be done.

Most of these so-called marketing firms are of little or no value to the independent inventor. Virtually all of the firms reviewed offer the three services listed below plus drafting and other clerical services thrown in as a part of the package.

Some of the fees are reasonable for the work performed and some are inflated—it depends on the firm. What's more important is whether you need the services. Let's look at what they're proposing and what it is that you need.

Statistical Analysis Figures

Of all the crap, con jobs, and hype I've ever experienced in my life, this has got to be the worst of them all.

I grew up with statistical analysis as a way of life. My mother spent over 20 years working for Gallup Poll and Mervin Field Research. These are two of the largest and most reputable firms in the world for conducting statistical analysis profiles and reports. They'll both tell you the same things:

- Statistics can be manipulated—the answers you get depend on the questions you ask and how you ask them. Trained professionals who can be objective with the analysis of the data must do the work if you want accuracy.

- Given enough statistics, you can prove ANYTHING you want to.

- If the statistics you gather don't tell you what you want to hear, gather some more statistics that do.

What does this mean to an independent inventor? Simple—don't believe a whole bunch of statistics about the marketing potential for your invention that come from an invention marketing company.

They generally don't know anything about your invention or the market you're targeting so they're not qualified to make an analysis or give you any recommendations—positive or negative.

Here's a perfect example of what I'm talking about:

Let's say that you've invented a new board game that all your friends and family like. An invention marketing company goes through a computer database of statistical information (these examples are mythical) and comes up with the following statistics:

- There are 157,765 stores and retail outlets that sell board games.

- In the past five years, 6,497,576 board games have been sold in the US.

- The potential market for your game is over 100,000 stores and over 5 million game players in the US alone.

The statistics are true but are they of any value? No, they are not because they only address the potential market for board games. Nothing that was reported has anything specifically to do with your new game other than the fact that it's a board game.

All they're doing is providing a historical record of what's happened in the past. There is absolutely nothing involved here that tells you anything about the future of your game.

NONE of these firms (ours included) can tell you what the ultimate marketing and sales potentials of your game are because they are not in the business of marketing board games. Logically, only the companies who are currently manufacturing and marketing products in your target market have any true knowledge of what's going on because their very survival depends on it, and sometime even they're wrong.

Now here's a logical question; *"Since the firms who are currently manufacturing and marketing products in your area of invention know what's going on, wouldn't it make sense to solicit their opinions about your invention?"*

If you answered yes, you understand why this is the only sensible thing to do—locate and solicit the firms that are currently successful at manufacturing and marketing the kinds of products you invented.

There is another avenue of evaluation that makes sense too, but it deviates a little from the rest of the book—it involves letting a pure marketing company evaluate your idea.

Pure marketing firms are organizations like the Home Shopping Network, catalog companies like Lillian Vernon and Walter Drake, and producers of successful television commercials like Ron Popeil of Ronco with his Pasta Machine and Bob Klayman, of Media Innovations Inc., the man who promoted the Ginsu knives into a 100 million dollar product.

These are multimillion dollar per quarter firms with a track record of success in marketing all kinds of products and innovations. Their continued success depends on their ability to recognize new items that they believe the public will pay for.

If you can get one of these firms to evaluate your ideas and inventions from the standpoint of marketability, you've probably got a pretty good idea of whether you've got a profit making product or not.

Patent Applications

If you haven't read the section on patenting yet, go back and read it first before you go any farther. I've done my best to explain to you why patenting may or may not be important to your ultimate marketing and profit making success.

The invention marketing firms usually rely on your lack of understanding, misunderstanding, or outright ignorance of the patent process and start out by trying to convince you that you can't even consider going to market without a patent. I've even heard of cases where inventors have been told that it was illegal to market their products without a patent.

Most of the invention marketing firms are under heavy investigation by the State Attorney Generals for fraud and misrepresentation.

If you need a patent, obtain the services of a licensed officer of the court (a patent attorney) and check out their reputation for getting the job done right for the fees that they quote.

Advertising Your Inventions

Here's the hype: *"We guarantee to submit your invention to all 500 of the Fortune 500 companies four times in the next year!"*

Sounds impressive, doesn't it? Based on research, they all follow the letter of the law and do exactly what the guarantee says they will do.

Here's the problem summed up in three questions:

1. How many of the Fortune 500 companies are viable candidates to handle your product?

2. What are the invention marketing companies sending these companies in the way of literature, and other related marketing materials?

3. Who are they actually sending the material to other than the mailroom to be dumped with the other junk mail?

If these questions lead you to believe that what they do follows the letter of the law but in the process of licensing an invention are completely worthless, you're not alone.

Countless inventors have been bilked out of tens of millions of dollars by these firms because they thought that the invention marketing firms was actually doing something worthwhile in terms of promoting their inventions.

Here's where I get to stand on my soapbox and tell you a little about my past. In the late 1970's, I was the Director of Engineering for a division of one of the Fortune 500 companies.

The company was Notifier Corporation who you probably recognize as the one who manufactures and markets burglar alarms, smoke detectors, security systems, and a whole line of related products.

I even hold the patent on the Coded Security System or what you'd call a wireless burglar alarm system. (It's US Patent number 4,257,038 if you want to look it up.)

After I left that job, I took over as Vice President of Engineering and Operations for Entex, a $65 million per year toy manufacturer. We were the firm that produced the handheld versions of most of the popular arcade games like Space Invaders, Pac Man, Galaxian, Crazy Climber, Turtles, and dozens of others.

Later on, I was one of the people who helped set up Worlds of Wonder, the toy company that manufactured Teddy Ruxpin, the computerized teddy bear that has made the inventors over $68 million in royalties.

During my years in these positions, I was involved in the licensing of dozens of products that made millions of dollars for the inventors. That's the good news. The bad news is that we NEVER went looking for these inventions— they always came looking for us! If you don't understand what this means, I'll explain it in more detail.

None of these firms, all of whom were in the business of licensing new inventions, went looking for the new inventions in either the patent room of the library or in ANY kind of a newsletter or publication that advertised inventions for sale. It didn't make sense for us to look at stuff that wasn't of any interest to us because we had better things to do with our time.

On the other hand, when a toy inventor, for example, would send us information directly, we'd ALWAYS look at it to see if it was something that we might want to consider adding to our new line of products.

That's where we got our new ideas and it's where other companies get theirs too—not from some journal with hundreds or thousands of nondescript inventions listed by name and patent number. We needed specific details before we preceded any farther and these generic lists of inventions don't provide it.

Furthermore, most major manufacturers would NEVER do business with any of these invention marketing firms if they were acting as your agent because of the status and reputation of the firms. It's too risky.

What a manufacturer or potential licensee is looking for is a direct conduit to the inventor and/or your specific representative—not some questionable firm who is under investigation by the State Attorney General.

The simple conclusion is that your best bet is to prepare your own materials and directly solicit the types of firms that are likely candidate to manufacture and market your inventions. Period!

So, what's it all mean? Should you NOT get involved with anybody who's offering to help you with obtaining success with your inventions? NO! Of course not! But I am saying that you MUST be careful about where you put your time and money. Look carefully at what you need to do, or have done, in order to profitably get your invention to market.

Write down a plan of action that has three columns:

Column 1. Things that you need to profitably get your invention licensed.

Column 2. Those things that you can do yourself.

Column 3. Those things that would be better done by someone other than you.

Once you have this list, you have the instruction manual and all the steps required for you to find out if your idea is licensable or whether you should abandon it and work on something else. With this shopping list in hand, you can now confidently decide who is going to perform the necessary tasks and how much it's going to cost you.

If you hear any of these comments, I hope that you realize that they are stock phrases, which may be exactly what you had hoped to hear:

- "We think your idea has great market potential." Few ideas, however good, become commercially successful. (Look at the statistics in Chapter 1 starting on page 3). If a company fails to disclose that investing in your idea is a high-risk venture, and that most ideas never make any money, beware.

"It is a fact that less than one percent of all new product concepts succeed in the marketplace," said Jodie Bernstein, Director of the FTC's Bureau of Consumer Protection, at a press conference announcing Project Mousetrap. Yet the fraudulent firms in this industry conclude, after a *professional* evaluation, that virtually every new idea or product crossing their desks is patentable and has *tremendous market potential.*"

- "Our company has licensed invention ideas successfully." If a company tells you it has a good track record, ask for a list of its successful clients. Confirm that these clients have had commercial success. If the company refuses to give you a list of their successful clients, it probably means they don't have any.

- "You need to hurry and patent your idea before someone else does." Be wary of high-pressure sales tactics. Patenting your idea does NOT mean you will ever make any money from it.

- "Congratulations! We've done a patent search on your idea, and we have some great news. There's nothing like it out there." Many invention promotion firms claim to perform patent searches on ideas. Patent searches by fraudulent invention promotion firms usually are incomplete, conducted in the wrong category, or unaccompanied by a legal opinion on the results of the search from a patent attorney.

"Many unscrupulous firms agree in their contracts to identify manufacturers by coding your idea with the US Bureau of Standard Industrial Code (SIC). Lists of manufacturers that come from classifying your idea with the SIC usually are of limited value."

Because unscrupulous firms promote virtually any idea or invention without regard to its patentability, they may market an idea for which someone already has a valid, active patent. In that case, you may be the subject of a patent infringement lawsuit—even if the promotional efforts on your invention are successful.

- "Our research department, engineers and patent attorneys have evaluated your idea. We definitely want to move forward." This is a standard sales pitch. Many questionable firms do not perform any evaluation at all. In fact, many don't have the professional staff they claim.

- "Our company has evaluated your idea, and now wants to prepare a more in-depth research report. It'll be several hundred dollars." If the company's initial evaluation is positive, ask why the company isn't willing to cover the cost of researching your idea further.

- Our company makes most of its money from the royalties it gets from licensing its clients' ideas. Of course, we need some money from you before we get started. If a firm tells you this, but asks you for a large up front fee, ask why they're not willing to help you on a contingency basis.

Unscrupulous firms make almost all their money from large upfront fees. Virtually no consumers have even made back their investment, let alone any profit, from these companies' services.

The paperwork supplied is a travesty as well. The FTC has showed samples of the reports that are supplied to the inventors. They often are quite lengthy, but typically are mass-produced and consist largely of boilerplate pages into which the inventor's name and idea is electronically inserted.

Help Is On The Way

You're not alone in your world of inventing and the federal government is keenly aware of the problems that inventors are facing.

The FTC works for the consumer to prevent fraudulent, deceptive and unfair business practices and to provide information to help consumers spot, stop and avoid them. To file a complaint or to get free information on consumer issues, call toll free, 877-382-4357, or use the on-line complaint form.

To assist you in the process of inventing while not getting ripped-off, we've located the following resources that we believe are among the best around. There are, of course, hundreds of others, but we believe that if you look into these resources that you'll have over 80 percent of all the fraud prevention information you'll need to get on with your creativity without the fear of being ripped-off.

To check if a company has been investigated and/or fined by the Federal Trade Commission (FTC), enter the word INVENTION in the FTC's web site search engine (http://www.ftc.gov/search) and you will be able to view a list of FTC news releases about invention scam.

The USPTO has a great report on how to spot the scams and what to look for. You can read and print the entire report at http://www.inventorfraud.com/pto.pdf.

The Federal Trade Commission has found that many invention promotion firms claim, falsely, that they can turn ideas into cash. But, the agency says, smart inventors can learn to spot the sweet-sounding promises of a fraudulent promotion firm.

Copies of the complaints, as well as the consumer education materials, are available from the FTC's web site at http://www.ftc.gov and also from the FTC's Public Reference Branch, Room 130, 6th Street and Pennsylvania Ave NW, Washington, D.C. 20580; 202-326-2222.

You may want to visit the web site of the National Congress of Inventor Organizations at (http://www.inventionconvention.com/ncio.index.html).

A great place to start your education in successful inventing is http://www.patentcafe.com. It's a gathering place where professionals and new inventors, researchers and innovators, and kids and adults trade ideas or explore new thoughts and dreams.

PatentCafe serves a wide cross section of individuals and groups interested in intellectual property from international policymakers, to inventors and engineers, to kids and teachers, and constantly updates 1,000s of pages of content to match your interests including:

- Tuesday night expert chats
- Ask the Experts Forum
- Message board

- Advice from magazine editors
- Inventor events.

Another place to check out is http://www.tenonline.org/npw.html. This is actually a paper written by Ed Zimmer of The Entrepreneur Network about the realities and potentials for success as an independent inventor. It's not as upbeat an article as it could be, but it's certainly realistic about the current chances for success and the realities of the licensing process.

I've included it here as a second independent opinion to solidify the information in this book and reinforce the fact that this is a business and contains all of the hardships and heartaches of any business. In other words, although it's possible (and there are independent inventors every day who license their inventions), it's not a get rich quick scheme.

The one thing I definitely need to say about this article is that it's dated and that means that as the market changes, the possibilities and odds for success change as well. I was in the toy business when we had an open door policy and clamored for creative individuals, just like you, to bring us new ideas and innovations. Since then, that market has changed but others have opened their doors to creative individuals and their ideas.

Remember that the licensing process was pioneered by, and is still utilized by, the publishing industry that demands that independent writers submit their books drafts for consideration.

Anyone who has been successfully published will tell you that most of their friends, family, and business associates told them that they'd never be successful and to drop the idea of ever being published. Yet, in spite of that, they went ahead and collected dozens, perhaps hundreds of rejection slips and didn't give up until they found a publisher.

Of course, after they were published, the same people who told them it would never happen began to say "man you're lucky" when luck had nothing to do with it. The process was mechanics, not magic, and they were successful because of sheer determination and hard work.

The invention licensing process is the same way and any one who has been successful will tell you that it's a combination of creative thinking, determination, and most of all, persistence in the face of the best wishes of everyone around you.

Well that's it folks—the step-by-step procedure for finding a licensee (buyer) for your invention. The process might not have been exactly what you thought it would be but the information is both authentic and accurate. As I stated in the opening, inventors, inventions, and the opportunity to profit from them have been around since the cave dwellers and it'll continue to be with us forever.

Your place in this process as an inventor is to continue to be creative regardless of whether you become rich and famous. Look around the room where you're at right now. Everything started with a person, just like you, who had an idea, just like you, and decided to do something with it.

They probably had the same doubts, fears, and concerns that you do and went ahead and did something anyway. Now it's your turn—go and do something creative with your ideas and inventions and make the world that you and I both live in a better place to be.

If you're still not convinced of the potential of your creative genius, I've saved the most powerful statement I can think of for last.

In all the years I've been delivering my seminars to tens of thousands of inventors, I've never met one who showed their idea to someone and had it ripped-off. And yet, in all my years of delivering my seminars to tens of thousands of inventors, I've never met one who hadn't had one or more great ideas that they were "going to get around to" only to turn around one day and see it in the marketplace.

The truth is that if you wait around long enough someone else will come up with the same idea or solution to a problem and if they decide to make their move to the marketplace before you do, they're the ones who will profit—not you. I'm going to bet that you're one of those people who's seen their products on the shelf with someone else's name on it.

I've done my best in this book to show you the step-by-step process for profitably exploiting your ideas and inventions. All you have to do is step up to the plate and go get your own share of success.

Don't worry if you strike out a few times. Just remember that a 300 hitter in baseball strikes out 7 out of 10 times and still makes $5 million dollars a year. Now get out there and start swinging at the market so you can get your share of the profits as a reward for your creativity.

Appendix

American Society for Journalists and Authors
http://www.asja.org

An Intellectual Property Law Primer for Multimedia and Web Developers
http://www.eff.org/Censorship/Academic_edu/CAF/l aw/multimedia-handbook

Associated Press
50 Rockefeller Plaza
New York NY 10020
212-621-1500
http://www.AP.org

Edgar W. (Ted) Averill, Jr.
Averill and Varn
8244 Painter Avenue
Whittier CA 90602-3109
562-698-8039
Patent Attorney

Christian Copyright Licensing International (CCLI)
17201 NE Sacramento
Portland OR 97230
800-234-2446 x 315
http://www.ccli.com

Consumer Product Safety Commission
5401 Westbard Avenue
Bethesda MD 20816

Copyright Clearance Center (CCC)
222 Rosewood Drive
Danvers MA 01923
978-750-8400
http://www.copyright.com
mailto:info@copyright.com

Department of Health and Human Services
Public Health Service
Food and Drug Administration
5600 Fisher Lane Room #16-85
Rockville MD 20857-0002
FDA97-1229 Can Your Kitchen Pass The Food Safety Test?
FDA96-1260 Compilation of Laws Enforced by FDA Vol 1
FDA97-1167 Getting Information from FDA

Dream Merchant
John Morland
2309 Torrance Boulevard Suite 104
Torrance CA 90501
310-328-1925
http://www.dreammerchant.net
mailto:JKM316@aol.com
an inventor's newsletter/magazine

Electronic Industries Association
Consumer Electronics Group
2001 Eye Street Northwest
Washington DC 20006-1804

Environmental Protection Agency (EPA)
999 18th Street Suite 500
Denver CO 80202-2466
303-312-6312 General Information

Federal Communications Commission
Laboratory Division
PO Box 40
Laurel MD 20745-0040
FDA96-1092 Small Business Guide to FDA

Federal Trade Commission
Public Reference Room 130
200 7th St NW
Washington DC 20580-0002
202-326-2222
Public Reference/Information Specialist
http://www.ftc.gov/
A Guide to the Federal Trade Commission
Infomercials
Special Contracts
Warranties
Invention Promotion Firms

Invention Convention
Administrative & Communications Center
PO Box 931881
Los Angeles CA 90093-6690
323-460-4408
http://www.inventionconvention.com
mailto:inventionconvention@inventionconvention.com

Invention Place
National Inventors Hall of Fame
221 S Broadway
Akron OH 44308

Inventors Awareness Group
1533 East Mountain Rd Ste B
Westfield MA 01085-1458
mailto:iagbob@aol.com

Inventors' Digest
310 Franklin St Ste 24
Boston MA 02110
704-369-7312
mailto:InventorsD@aol.com
http://www.inventorsdigest.com
Subscription: $22 per year for bimonthly magazine

Marke Systems
Mark Moulding, President
2017 Lomita Blvd
Lomita CA 90717
800-557-7718 or 310-326-2753
310-326-6158 f
mailto:MARKESys@MARKESys.com

Oppedahl and Larson
http://www.patents.com

Dave Hatton
Plastic Molded Components, Inc.
5921 Lakeshore Drive
Cypress CA 90630
714-229-0133
plastic injection molding, plastic and die cast tooling

Product Design and Prototypes
Frank Speers
mailto:fspeers@microsys.net

Professional Photographers of America, Inc. (PPA)
229 Peachtree St NE Suite 2200
Atlanta GA 30303
404-522-8600 or 800-786-6277
http://www.PPA.com

Software & Information Industry Assoc
090 Vermont Ave NW Sixth Floor
Washington DC 20005
202-289-7442
800-388-7478
http://www.spa.org
To report software piracy

Stanford University Libraries
http://fairuse.stanford.edu

T2 Design & Prototyping
Paul Berman, President
1238 7th St
Santa Monica CA 90401-1606
310-656-9922
mailto:t2design@aol.com
http://t2inventions.com
product development

Ten Big Myths about copyrights
http://www.templetons.com/brad/copymyths.html

Thomson and Thomson
http://www.thomson-thomson.com

Toy Industry Association
200 Fifth Avenue Suite 740
New York NY 10010-3468
212-675-1141
www.Toy-TIA.org
toy inventor guide available online

Trade Show Resource
PO Box 6511
Holliston MA 01746
mailto:info@tsnn.com
http://www.TSNN.com

Underwriters Laboratories Inc.
Corporate Headquarters
333 Pfingsten Road
Northbrook IL 60062-2096
http://www.ul.com/

Register of Copyrights
US Copyright Office
Library of Congress
Washington DC 20559-6000
202-707-3000
202-707-5959 information 8:30 am to 5:00 pm
Census Office of Public Affairs

US Department of Commerce
Federal Office Building No 3
Room 2705
Washington DC 20233

National Bureau of Standards
US Department of Commerce
A903 Administration Building
Washington DC 20234
301-975-2758 [Business Affairs Office)

National Institute of Standards and Technology (NIST)
US Department of Commerce
Publications and Programs Inquiries
Gaithersburg MD 20899-0001
301-975-3058 Public and Business Affairs Div
mailto:inquiries@nist.gfov
http://www.nist.gov

Office of Consumer Affairs
US Department of Commerce
808 17th Street NW Suite 800
Washington DC 20006
http://www.doc.gov/
mailto:CAffairs@doc.gov
Consumer's Resource Handbook

US Patent and Trademark Office
2121 Crystal Drive Suite 0100
Arlington VA 22202-3661
800-786-9199 automated information messages
http://www.uspto.gov/

Index

PRODUCT CATALOG

The 99¢ Gourmet™

Includes the basics you'll need to make sure that you eat well for less including over 120 pages of useful information to cut your food bills by 40 percent by applying guidelines to change the way you purchase and prepare the foods you eat.

Book   ISBN 978-1-891440-60-1   **$29.95**

Book Marketing for the Clueless®

Want to sell your books, CDs and DVDs for a profit? This audio/PDF CD includes databases of over 500 catalogs and outlets that market books and instructions on how to solicit your publications including how to be listed with Amazon.com for free.

Audio/Data CD⁺   ISBN 978-1-891440-49-6   **$24.95**

Clutterology® Getting Rid of Clutter and Getting Organized!

A complete manual on how to get organized, set up and maintain manageable filing systems, and eliminate clutter that gets in your way. Provides some of the simplest, easiest and most practical advice on how to remove the clutter from your life and get organized.

Book   ISBN 978-1-891440-62-5   **$34.95**
eBook*   ISBN 978-1-891440-71-7   **$10.00**

Clutterology® Eliminate the Clutter in Your Life and Get Organized!

Companion to the Clutterology book, the information in this 3 DVD set will help you to adapt your home and work environment to your style and attitude. Recorded in-studio and contains a combination of lecture and actual demonstrations using dozens of common implements found in stores to organize, clean, and reduce clutter.

DVD   ISBN 978-1-891440-61-8   **$39.95**

Highlights of Clutterology®

This audio CD has over 60 minutes of tips, tricks, insights, and stories about getting rid of your clutter and getting organized. It's ideal for reinforcement to remind you that getting organized is a step-by-step process that you can accomplish if you take it easy and stick with it.

Audio CD⁺   ISBN 978-1-891440-50-2   **$19.95**

How to Become a Clutterologist™

Do label makers and shelf dividers make you smile? Use your aptitude for organization to change lives and turn your decluttering skills into a moneymaking career; become a professional organizer! Includes the tools and knowledge you need to succeed in the professional organizer industry: organizing specialties, understanding the Clutter-Hoarding Scale, how to structure your business for SUCCESS, business licensing and insurance.

Book   ISBN 978-1-891440-56-4   **$29.95**
eBook*   ISBN 978-1-891440-68-7   **$10.00**

Contracts and Agreements for Inventors

Two dozen of the most utilized agreements to help ensure that what's yours stays yours. With the help of an attorney, they contain everything you'll need from a confidentiality agreement to work-for-hire agreements, assignment of rights, and partnership agreements. Comes with instructions for usage, filling out, and filing where applicable.

Data CD⁺   **$19.95**

***All eBooks contain a complete book in PDF format on a single CD for use on Macintosh and Windows computers.**
⁺**All data files are in PDF format, playable/viewable on Windows and Mac, audio files are in Wave format playable on standard CD players.**

Fishin' With A Net

Learn the elements of designing a Web site that actually works for you and can be created in less than four hours. Covers what the Web really is, what to put on your site to be successful, and how to link with the search engines quickly and easily.

Book ISBN 978-1-891440-55-7 **$24.95**
eBook* ISBN 978-1-891440-42-7 **$10.00**

Goin' Pro

If you want to be a professional speaker, this program, recorded live at the Toastmasters International Convention will show you three ways you make money in the speaking business: how to work for seminar companies, ways to market yourself and how to create written products for back-of-room sales.

DVD **$19.95**

Headline Creator™ Pro Suite

"Your headline can result in 80 percent or more of the effectiveness of your ad or sales page!" Automatically generates time-tested, proven, results-oriented headlines based on the greatest headlines in history...and does it in 17 seconds!

Windows Software CD **$19.95**

Home Business Tax Savings Made Easy!

The average home business owner is overpaying taxes by at least $20.00 a day because of what they don't know. You'll learn the big tax breaks available to home-based business owners, exactly how to qualify for each of them, and how to easily keep bullet-proof tax records.

Book ISBN 0-9707538-9-6 **$37.00**

How to Develop an Effective Web Site

Self-running CD takes you through the process of creating Web sites and getting them posted on the Web. Includes over 130 narrated slides with complete details and explanations on everything from renting a domain name cheaply to getting a shopping cart for FREE!

Data CD⁺ ISBN 978-1-891440-43-4 **$19.95**

How To Sell Your Inventions for Cash

Everything you need to know to be a successful inventor! Takes your idea from inception through the licensing process to a manufacturer for royalties. Learn how to protect your inventions using patents, trademarks, copyrights, and other legal instruments, determine if you're ready to offer your idea, and how to find and solicit manufacturers who are interested in your ideas.

Book ISBN 978-1-891440-27-4 **$24.95**
eBook* ISBN 978-1-891440-69-4 **$10.00**
Audio CD⁺ ISBN 978-1-891440-28-1 **$39.95**

Intellectual Property Protection for the Clueless®

CD contains 3 hours of audio plus 100s of pages in PDF format on trademarks, patents and copyright. Includes forms for filing without an attorney! *Bonus: How to Apply for an Innovation Research Grant!* This audio is in MP3 format playable with the Widows Media Player or comparable MP3 software.

MP3 Audio/Data CD⁺ ISBN 978-1-891440-67-0 **$59.95**

Marketing for the Clueless®

The process of successful marketing is mechanics – not magic, and the mechanics have been simply explained to apply to all your needs. You'll learn the seven elements of marketing, how they apply to you and how to create a marketing plan that actually works for you.

Audio/Data CD⁺ ISBN 978-1-891440-54-0 **$24.95**

*All eBooks contain a complete book in PDF format on a single CD for use on Macintosh and Windows computers.
+All data files are in PDF format, playable/viewable on Windows and Mac, audio files are in Wave format playable on standard CD players.

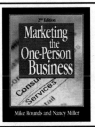

Marketing the One-Person Business

A one-person business is different from any other because you have to do the business PLUS get the business. Contains complete information about setup, operation, independent contractor criteria and forms, fee setting, consulting, public speaking, seminars, contracts and agreements.

Book ISBN 978-1-891440-29-8 *$24.95*

eBook * ISBN 978-1-891440-41-0 *$10.00*

Marketing with Postcards

The most cost effective way to promote any product or service is with postcards. You'll learn how to design a GOOD marketing postcard that gets response, how to effectively evaluate your postcards before printing, and resources for low-cost postcard layout and printing.

DVD ISBN 978-1-891440-34-2 *$39.95*

Mechanics of Staring a Home-Based Business

A home-based business is a business whose primary office is in the owner's home. Explains the realities of starting and operating a home business and including resources for taxes, licenses, and advertising plus computer operated business you can start and run.

Book ISBN 978-1-891440-63-2 *$34.95*

eBook * ISBN 978-1-891440-70-0 *$10.00*

Mining the College Market

Local colleges provide hundreds of millions of dollars in revenues each year and are responsible for well over 200,000 paid training programs each year. Contains a 212 page manual with complete resources plus a three hour seminar on auto run CD, complete with narrative and slides plus a special edition of Self Publishing for the Clueless®.

Book and CD⁺ *$399.00*

Missing Tools Software Suite

Web site add-ons: Site search engine, Misspelling Generator that creates misspelled keywords to help overcome inability of searchers to correctly spell your meta-tags, Thumbnail Tool provides batch thumbnailing for images, and Slideshow Maker converts multiple views and turns still images into a self-running slide show presentation.

Windows Software CD *$79.95*

Name Razor™

The ultimate naming software utility that uses a database of hundreds of *namelets*, to quickly create thousands of potential name ideas in minutes! It'll help you with domain names, company name, info products, brands... and more.

Windows Software CD *$19.95*

Professional Speaking for the Clueless®

Do you want to be paid to speak? Explains the REAL business of professional speaking and how to make six figures a year without huge marketing and advertising costs. Includes dozens of resources, databases, and complete explanations of how to locate speaking opportunities and market to them.

Audio/Data CD⁺ ISBN 978-1-891440-53-3 *$24.95*

Profitable Publishing for the Clueless®

The complete 3 CD set containing everything you need to know to generate, protect, and market your printed work. See full description for each item.

Disk 1 - Self-Publishing for the Clueless®
Disk 2 - Trademarks & Copyrights for the Clueless®
Disk 3 - Book Marketing for the Clueless®

Audio/Data CD⁺ ISBN 978-1-891440-51-9 *$59.95*

All eBooks contain a complete book in PDF format on a single CD for use on Macintosh and Windows computers.
+All data files are in PDF format, playable/viewable on Windows and Mac, audio files are in Wave format playable on standard CD players.

Project Management for the Clueless®

Organizing and managing projects doesn't have to be complicated and effective project management doesn't take a long time to learn – just a simple explanation of what needs to be done and why! This CD will show you how to organize, budget, and manage projects in three hours or less.

Audio/Data CD⁺ ISBN 978-1-891440-37-3 **$24.95**

Self-Publishing for the Clueless®

You can write and publish your own book for less than $3.00 per copy, in less than 90 days. Contains complete information, examples, and resources for everything you'll need including get bar codes, cover designs, and low-cost printing sources.

Audio/Data CD⁺ ISBN 978-1-891440-36-6 **$24.95**

Speakers/Publishers Support Material

Contains software including Acoustica™, Audacity™ Audio Recorders, Label Maker, PDF software and Microsoft Producer®. Comes complete with narration and special effects and a Tips Booklet Template® that can be used as a cut and paste model for your own tips booklet.

Windows Software and Data CD **$39.95**

Talk, Talk, Talk

A 2½ hour DVD that shows you how to speak for free and make money on the luncheon circuit, present seminars and workshops at local colleges and how to get on talk radio shows sell products and promote yourself into a nationally recognized expert.

DVD ISBN 978-1-891440-48-9 **$39.95**

Trademarks & Copyrights for the Clueless®

Trademarks are the mark of your trade and Copyrights address the laws allowing you the rights to make copies of your work. Contains printable forms and examples, explaining how to protect your works plus what material of others you can use without fear of legal problems.

Audio/Data CD⁺ ISBN 978-1-891440-30-4 **$24.95**

Venture Capital for the Clueless®

Venture capital is available for all types of businesses and your ability to tap into it depends on your ability to write a business plan that sells you and your ideas to the people with the money. Includes explanations, samples, printable forms, and sources of venture funding.

Audio/Data CD⁺ ISBN 978-1-891440-31-1 **$24.95**

VideoWeb Wizard™

Software suite to convert your audio and video recordings to Flash™ format for fast and efficient downloads of audio and video on your Web site. Includes VideoWeb Wizard™ software and tutorial, Flash Audio Wizard™, Audacity™ Audio Recording and Editing software plus bonus programs.

Windows Software CD **$99.95**

Whadda We Do NOW?™

Provides quick fixes for failing businesses. Learn how to quickly and easily figure out what's wrong so you can stop guessing and start implementing solutions. The information is practical, easy to understand, and readily implementable if you're serious about getting your business into a positive cash flow position-NOW!

Book ISBN 978-1-891440-66-3 **$29.95**

All eBooks contain a complete book in PDF format on a single CD for use on Macintosh and Windows computers.
All data files are in PDF format, playable/viewable on Windows and Mac, audio files are in Wave format playable on standard CD players.

Training Kits

Become a Professional Organizer

If you'd like to get into the lucrative world of professional organizing, then everything you'll need to setup a business, get clients, and operate profitably is on the list below. Contains:

Books: How to Become a Clutterologist™, Clutterology® Getting Rid of Clutter and Getting Organized! Mechanics of Starting a Home-Based Business, and Marketing the One-Person Business.

Plus DVD/CDs: Headline Creator™ Pro Suite, How to Develop an Effective Web Site, Marketing with Postcards, Profitable Publishing for the Clueless®, and Clutterology® Eliminate the Clutter in Your Life and Get Organized!

Kit $261.95

Entrepreneurship

Do you dream of working for yourself? This kit includes everything for setting up a home based business, getting organized, raising venture capital to fund the efforts, scheduling and managing your time, and ways to market your skills profitably. Contains:

Books: Mechanics of Starting a Home-Based Business, Marketing the One-Person Business, Clutterology® Getting Rid of Clutter and Getting Organized! and How to Develop an Effective Web Site.

Plus DVD/CDs: Headline Creator™ Pro Suite, Speakers/Publishers Support Materials, Marketing with Postcards, Project Management for the Clueless®, Marketing for the Clueless®, Professional Speaking for the Clueless®, Profitable Publishing for the Clueless®, and Venture Capital for the Clueless®.

Kit $169.95

Invention Marketing

The material listed is endorsed by the SBA as "The only legitimate program for marketing inventions that we've ever seen." It explains how to organize and manage your invention process, protect them with patents, trademarks and copyrights, set up a home business, offer your ideas for sale, plus information for raising venture capital to fund your projects. Contains:

Books: How to Sell Your Inventions for Cash and Mechanics of Starting a Home-Based Business.

Plus DVD/CDs: How to Sell Your Inventions for Cash, Contracts and Agreements for Inventors, Venture Capital for the Clueless®, Project Management for the Clueless®, and Trademarks & Copyrights for the Clueless®.

Kit $161.95

Marketing

Your business has two parts: getting the business and doing the business. If you're like most people, you're probably very good at doing the business but unsure about being able to get the business. This kit of materials will help you get past the problems of "getting" the business including materials for creating headlines, writing advertising copy, and locating low-cost, high profit ways to promote your business. Contains:

Book: Marketing the One-Person Business.

Plus DVD/CDs: Marketing for the Clueless®, Profitable Publishing for the Clueless®, Marketing with Postcards, Headline Creator™ Pro Suite, and How to Develop an Effective Web Site.

Kit $191.95

Professional Speaking

If you're interested in professional speaking, you'll find everything needed to get profitable bookings including places to get booked and instructions on how to do it! Includes over 1,700 pages of printable information, eight hours of video, four hours of audio, and hundreds of support resources. Contains:

Books: Mining the College Market (plus CDs), Marketing the One-Person Business, Mechanics of Starting A Home-Based Business, andFishin' with a Net.

Plus DVD/CDs: Headline Creator™ Pro Suite, Speakers/Publishers Support Material, Marketing with Postcards, Talk, Talk, Talk, Project Management for the Clueless®, Marketing for the Clueless®, Professional Speaking for the Clueless®, and Profitable Publishing for the Clueless®.

Kit $261.95

All eBooks contain a complete book in PDF format on a single CD for use on Macintosh and Windows computers.
All data files are in PDF format, playable/viewable on Windows and Mac, audio files are in Wave format playable on standard CD players.

Raising Venture Capital

Looking for money or backing for a new idea or enterprise? Confused about what to do and how to approach investors? We've assembled the materials needed to establish proprietary rights to your innovations; plan, budget, organize and schedule your project; prepare a business plan and shop it to people with investment capital. Contains:

Books: Clutterology® Getting Rid of Clutter and Getting Organized! and Mechanics of Starting a Home-Based Business.

Plus DVD/CDs: Trademarks & Copyrights for the Clueless®, Venture Capital for the Clueless®, Project Management for the Clueless®, Marketing for the Clueless®, Profitable Publishing for the Clueless®, Headline Creator™ Pro Suite, How to Develop an Effective Web Site, Marketing with Postcards, Clutterology® Eliminate the Clutter in Your Life and Get Organized!

Kit $191.95

Self-Publishing

You CAN have a book ready to sell in 30 days with these practical products...guaranteed! Contains everything needed including pre-configured scheduling and budgeting charts to get your own project finished in record time with a minimal amount of expense and hassles. Contains:

Books: Mechanics of Starting A Home-Based Business, and Fishin' With A Net.

Plus DVD/CDs: Self-Publishing for the Clueless®, Trademarks & Copyrights for the Clueless®, Book Marketing for the Clueless®, Marketing for the Clueless®, Headline Creator™ Pro Suite, Marketing with Postcards, and Project Management for the Clueless®.

Kit $261.95

Web Site Development Software Suite

No software you use to create your Web site will contain everything you need, so we've assembled the "stuff they left out." This suite of software and resources will help make your Web site work efficiently and get the response it deserves. These products have a proven track record in the world of Web design, marketing and advertising. Contains:

DVD/CDs: Video Web Wizard™, Flash Audio Web Wizard™, Headline Creator™ Pro Suite, Marketing With Postcards, Zoom-Your own Site Search Engine, Typo-Misspelling Generator, Image Thumbnail Resizer and Flash Slideshow Maker.

Kit $100.00

All eBooks contain a complete book in PDF format on a single CD for use on Macintosh and Windows computers.
+All data files are in PDF format, playable/viewable on Windows and Mac, audio files are in Wave format playable on standard CD players.

Rev. 1-10   Catalog Pg. 6

"Business and Technology Training Specialists"

6318 Ridgepath Court • Rancho Palos Verdes, CA 90275-3248
Telephone: (310) 544-9502 Fax (310) 544-3017 • www.RoundsMiller.com

ORDER FORM

ITEM (See Catalog for Full Description)	Format	Qty.	Price
The 99¢ Gourmet™	Book $29.95		
Book Marketing for the Clueless®	Audio/Data CD $24.95		
Clutterology® Getting Rid of Clutter and Getting Organized!	Book $34.95		
	eBook $10.00		
Clutterology® Eliminate the Clutter in Your Life and Get Organized!	DVD $39.95		
Highlights of Clutterology®	Audio CD $19.95		
How to Become a Clutterologist™	Book $29.95		
	eBook $10.00		
Contracts and Agreements for Inventors	Data CD $19.95		
Fishin' With A Net	Book $24.95		
	eBook $10.00		
Goin' Pro	DVD $19.95		
Headline Creator™ Pro Suite	Software CD $19.95		
Home Business Tax Savings Made Easy!	Book $37.00		
How to Develop an Effective Web Site	Data CD $19.95		
How To Sell Your Inventions for Cash	Book $24.95		
	eBook $10.00		
	Audio CD $39.95		
Intellectual Property Protection for the Clueless®	MP3 Audio/Data CD $59.95		
Marketing for the Clueless®	Audio/Data CD $24.95		
Marketing the One-Person Business	Book $24.95		
	eBook $10.00		
Marketing with Postcards	DVD $39.95		
Mechanics of Staring a Home-Based Business	Book $34.95		
	eBook $10.00		
Mining the College Market	Book and CD $399.00		
Missing Tools Software Suite	Software CD $79.95		
Name Razor™	Software CD $19.95		
Professional Speaking for the Clueless®	Audio/Data CD $24.95		
Profitable Publishing for the Clueless®	Audio/Data CD $59.95		
Project Management for the Clueless®	Audio/Data CD $24.95		
Self-Publishing for the Clueless®	Audio/Data CD $24.95		
Speakers/Publishers Support Material	Software/Data CD $39.95		
Talk, Talk, Talk	DVD $39.95		
Trademarks & Copyrights for the Clueless®	Audio/Data CD $24.95		
Venture Capital for the Clueless®	Audio/Data CD $24.95		
VideoWeb Wizard™	Software CD $99.95		
Whadda We Do NOW?™	Book $29.95		

		Page 1	**Sub-Total**	

Become a Professional Organizer	*Kit $261.95*		
Entrepreneurship	*Kit $169.95*		
Invention Marketing	*Kit $161.95*		
Marketing	*Kit $191.95*		
Professional Speaking	*Kit $261.95*		
Raising Venture Capital	*Kit $191.95*		
Self-Publishing	*Kit $261.95*		
Web Site Development Software Suite	*Kit $100.00*		

Amount from Page 1	
Sub-Total	
in CA add Sales Tax 9.25%	
Shipping	**$2.95**
Total	

Thank You!

Name (please print) _____

Mailing Address: _____

City, State, ZIP: _____

Tel: _____ e-Mail: _____

I authorize Rounds, Miller and Associates to charge my credit card for the items listed above

Credit Card Number: _____ exp. _____ CSS_____

Signature: _____ Date: _____

(If different than above)

Name on Card:_____

Statement Address: _____

City, State, ZIP: _____

To Order By Mail:

Send completed order form and check payable to Rounds, Miller and Associates to

6318 Ridgepath Court

Rancho Palos Verdes, CA 90275

To Order By Fax:

Fax both pages of completed order form with credit card info to Rounds, Miller and Associates

Fax (310) 544-3017